C000195094

THE PLAY
J. M. BARRIE

WHAT EVERY

WOMAN KNOWS

A COMEDY

CHARLES SCRIBNER'S SONS

NEW YORK : : : : : : : : : 1918

COPYRIGHT, 1918, BY
J. M. BARRIE

———

*All rights reserved under the International Copyright Act.
Performance forbidden and right of representation reserved.
Application for the right of performing this play must be
made to Charles Frohman, Inc., Empire Theatre, New York.*

I

*James Wylie is about to make a move on the dambrod,
and in the little Scotch room there is an awful silence
befitting the occasion. James with his hand poised—
for if he touches a piece he has to play it, Alick will
see to that—raises his red head suddenly to read
Alick's face. His father, who is Alick, is pretending
to be in a panic lest James should make this move.
James grins heartlessly, and his fingers are about to
close on the 'man' when some instinct of self-pre-
servation makes him peep once more. This time Alick
is caught: the unholy ecstasy on his face tells as
plain as porridge that he has been luring James to
destruction. James glares; and, too late, his opponent
is a simple old father again. James mops his head,
sprawls in the manner most conducive to thought in
the Wylie family, and, protruding his underlip,
settles down to a reconsideration of the board. Alick
blows out his cheeks, and a drop of water settles on
the point of his nose.*

*You will find them thus any Saturday night (after
family worship, which sends the servant to bed);*

1

and sometimes the pauses are so long that in the end they forget whose move it is.

It is not the room you would be shown into if you were calling socially on Miss Wylie. The drawing-room for you, and Miss Wylie in a coloured merino to receive you; very likely she would exclaim, 'This is a pleasant surprise!' though she has seen you coming up the avenue and has just had time to whip the dust-cloths off the chairs, and to warn Alick, David and James, that they had better not dare come in to see you before they have put on a dickey. Nor is this the room in which you would dine in solemn grandeur if invited to drop in and take pot-luck, which is how the Wylies invite, it being a family weakness to pretend that they sit down in the dining-room daily. It is the real living room of the house, where Alick, who will never get used to fashionable ways, can take off his collar and sit happily in his stocking soles, and James at times would do so also; but catch Maggie letting him.

There is one very fine chair, but, heavens, not for sitting on; just to give the room a social standing in an emergency. It sneers at the other chairs with an air of insolent superiority, like a haughty bride who has married into the house for money. Otherwise the furniture is homely; most of *it has come from that smaller house where the Wylies began. There is the large and shiny chair which can be turned into a bed if you look the other way for a moment. James cannot sit on this chair without gradually sliding down it till he is lying luxuriously on the small of his back, his legs indicating, like the hands of a clock, that it is ten past twelve; a position in which Maggie shudders to see him receiving company.*

The other chairs are horse-hair, than which nothing is more comfortable if there be a good slit down the seat. The seats are heavily dented, because all the Wylie family sit down with a dump. The draught-board is on the edge of a large centre table, which also displays four books placed at equal distances from each other, one of them a Bible, and another the family album. If these were the only books they would not justify Maggie in calling this chamber the library, her dogged name for it: while David and James call it the west-room and Alick calls it 'the room,' which is to him the natural name for any apart-ment without a bed in it. There is a bookcase of pitch pine, which contains six hundred books, with glass doors to prevent your getting at them.

No one does try to get at the books, for the Wylies are not a reading family. They like you to gasp when you see so much literature gathered together in one prison-house, but they gasp themselves at the thought that there are persons, chiefly clergymen, who, having finished one book, coolly begin another. Nevertheless it was not all vainglory that made David buy this library: it was rather a mighty respect for education, as something that he has missed. This same feeling makes him take in the Contemporary Review *and stand up to it like a man. Alick, who also has a respect for education, tries to read the* Contemporary, *but becomes dispirited, and may be heard muttering over its pages, 'No, no use, no use, no,' and sometimes even 'Oh hell.' James has no respect for education; and Maggie is at present of an open mind.*

They are Wylie and Sons of the local granite quarry, in which Alick was throughout his working days a mason. It is David who has raised them to this position; he climbed up himself step by step (and hewed the steps), and drew the others up after him. 'Wylie Brothers,' Alick would have had the firm called, but David said No, and James said No, and Maggie said No; first honour must be to their father; and Alick now likes it on the whole, though he often sighs at having to shave every day; and on some snell mornings he still creeps from his couch at four and even at two (thinking that his mallet and chisel are calling him), and begins to pull on his trousers, until the grandeur of them reminds him that he can go to bed again. Sometimes he cries a little, because there is no more work for him to do for ever and ever; and then Maggie gives him a spade (without telling David) or David gives him the logs to saw (without telling Maggie).

We have given James a longer time to make his move than our kind friends in front will give him, but in the meantime something has been happening. David has come in, wearing a black coat and his Sabbath boots, for he has been to a public meeting. David is nigh forty years of age, whiskered like his father and brother (Alick's whiskers being worn as a sort of cravat round the neck), and he has the too brisk manner of one who must arrive anywhere a little before any one else. The painter who did the three of them for fifteen pounds (you may observe the canvases on the walls) has caught this characteristic, perhaps accidentally, for David is almost stepping out of his frame, as if to hurry off somewhere; while Alick and James look as if they were pinned to the wall for life. All the six of them, men and pictures, however, have a family resemblance, like granite blocks from their own quarry. They are as Scotch as peat for instance, and they might exchange eyes without any neighbour noticing the difference, inquisi-

tive little blue eyes that seem to be always totting up the price of things.

The dambrod players pay no attention to David, nor does he regard them. Dumping down on the sofa he removes his 'lastic sides, as his Sabbath boots are called, by pushing one foot against the other, gets into a pair of hand-sewn slippers, deposits the boots as according to rule in the ottoman, and crosses to the fire. There must be something on David's mind to-night, for he pays no attention to the game, neither gives advice (than which nothing is more maddening) nor exchanges a wink with Alick over the parlous condition of James's crown. You can hear the wag-at-the-wall clock in the lobby ticking. Then David lets himself go; it runs out of him like a hymn:

DAVID. Oh, let the solid ground
        Not fail beneath my feet,
        Before my life has found
        What some have found so sweet.
        (This is not a soliloquy, but is offered as a definite statement. The players emerge from their game with difficulty.)

ALICK *(with* JAMES'S *crown in his hand).* What 's that you 're saying, David?

DAVID (*like a public speaker explaining the situation in a few well chosen words*). The thing I 'm speaking about is Love.

JAMES (*keeping control of himself*). Do you stand there and say you 're in love, David Wylie?

DAVID. Me; what would I do with the thing?

JAMES (*who is by no means without pluck*). I see no necessity for calling it a thing.

> (*They are two bachelors who all their lives have been afraid of nothing but Woman.* DAVID *in his sportive days—which continue—has done roguish things with his arm when conducting a lady home under an umbrella from a soiree, and has both chuckled and been scared on thinking of it afterwards.* JAMES, *a commoner fellow altogether, has discussed the sex over a glass, but is too canny to be in the company of less than two young women at a time.*)

DAVID (*derisively*). Oho, has she got you, James?

JAMES (*feeling the sting of it*). Nobody has got me.

DAVID.   They 'll catch you yet, lad.

JAMES.   They 'll never catch me.   You 've been nearer catched yourself.

ALICK.   Yes, Kitty Menzies, David.

DAVID (*feeling himself under the umbrella*). It was a kind of a shave that.

ALICK (*who knows all that is to be known about women and can speak of them without a tremor*). It 's a curious thing, but a man cannot help winking when he hears that one of his friends has been catched.

DAVID.   That 's so.

JAMES (*clinging to his manhood*).   And fear of that wink is what has kept the two of us single men.   And yet what 's the glory of being single?

DAVID.   There 's no particular glory in it, but it 's safe.

JAMES (*putting away his aspirations*).   Yes, it 's lonely, but it 's safe.   But who did you mean the poetry for, then?

DAVID.   For Maggie, of course.

(*You don't know* DAVID *and* JAMES *till you know how they love their sister* MAGGIE.)

ALICK. I thought that.

DAVID (*coming to the second point of his statement about Love*). I saw her reading poetry and saying those words over to herself.

JAMES. She has such a poetical mind.

DAVID. Love. There's no doubt as that's what Maggie has set her heart on. And not merely love, but one of those grand noble loves; for though Maggie is undersized she has a passion for romance.

JAMES (*wandering miserably about the room*). It's terrible not to be able to give Maggie what her heart is set on.

> (*The others never pay much attention to* JAMES, *though he is quite a smart figure in less important houses.*)

ALICK (*violently*). Those idiots of men.

DAVID. Father, did you tell her who had got the minister of Galashiels?

ALICK (*wagging his head sadly*). I had to tell her. And then I—I—bought her a sealskin muff, and I just slipped it into her hands and came away.

JAMES (*illustrating the sense of justice in the*

Wylie family). Of course, to be fair to the man, he never pretended he wanted her.

DAVID. None of them wants her; that's what depresses her. I was thinking, father, I would buy her that gold watch and chain in Snibby's window. She hankers after it.

JAMES (*slapping his pocket*). You're too late, David; I've got them for her.

DAVID. It's ill done of the minister. Many a pound of steak has that man had in this house.

ALICK. You mind the slippers she worked for him?

JAMES. I mind them fine; she began them for William Cathro. She's getting on in years, too, though she looks so young.

ALICK. I never can make up my mind, David, whether her curls make her look younger or older.

DAVID (*determinedly*). Younger. Whisht! I hear her winding the clock. Mind, not a word about the minister to her, James. Don't even mention religion this day.

JAMES. Would it be like me to do such a thing?

DAVID. It would be very like you. And there's that other matter: say not a syllable about our having a reason for sitting up late to-night. When she says it's bed-time, just all pretend we're not sleepy.

ALICK. Exactly, and when—

(*Here* MAGGIE *enters, and all three are suddenly engrossed in the dambrod. We could describe* MAGGIE *at great length. But what is the use? What you really want to know is whether she was good-looking. No, she was not. Enter* MAGGIE, *who is not good-looking. When this is said, all is said. Enter* MAGGIE, *as it were, with her throat cut from ear to ear. She has a soft Scotch voice and a more resolute manner than is perhaps fitting to her plainness; and she stops short at sight of* JAMES *sprawling unconsciously in the company chair.*)

MAGGIE. James, I wouldn't sit on the fine chair.

JAMES. I forgot again.

(*But he wishes she had spoken more sharply. Even profanation of the fine chair has not roused her. She takes up her knitting, and they all suspect that she knows what they have been talking about.*)

MAGGIE. You 're late, David, it 's nearly bed-time.

DAVID (*finding the subject a safe one*). I was kept late at the public meeting.

ALICK (*glad to get so far away from Galashiels*). Was it a good meeting?

DAVID. Fairish. (*With some heat.*) That young John Shand *would* make a speech.

MAGGIE. John Shand? Is that the student Shand?

DAVID. The same. It 's true he 's a student at Glasgow University in the winter months, but in summer he 's just the railway porter here; and I think it 's very presumptuous of a young lad like that to make a speech when he hasn't a penny to bless himself with.

ALICK. The Shands were always an impudent family, and jealous. I suppose that 's the reason they haven't been on speaking terms with us this six years. Was it a good speech?

DAVID (*illustrating the family's generosity*). It was very fine; but he needn't have made fun of *me*.

MAGGIE (*losing a stitch*). He dared?

DAVID (*depressed*). You see I can *not* get started on a speech without saying things like 'In rising *for* to make a few remarks.'

JAMES. What's wrong with it?

DAVID. He mimicked me, and said 'Will our worthy chairman come for to go for to answer my questions?' and so on; and they roared.

JAMES (*slapping his money pocket*). The sacket.

DAVID. I did feel bitterly, father, the want of education. (*Without knowing it, he has a beautiful way of pronouncing this noble word.*)

MAGGIE (*holding out a kind hand to him*). David.

ALICK I've missed it sore, David. Even now I feel the want of it in the very marrow of me. I'm shamed to think I never gave you your chance. But when you were young I was so desperate poor, how could I do it, Maggie?

MAGGIE. It wasn't possible, father.

ALICK (*gazing at the book-shelves*). To be able to understand these books! To up with them one at a time and scrape them as clean as though they were a bowl of brose. Lads, it's not to riches, it 's to scholarship that I make my humble bow.

JAMES (*who is good at bathos*). There 's ten yards of them. And they were selected by the minister of Galashiels. He said—

DAVID (*quickly*). James.

JAMES. I mean—I mean—

MAGGIE (*calmly*). I suppose you mean what you say, James. I hear, David, that the minister of Galashiels is to be married on that Miss Turnbull.

DAVID (*on guard*). So they were saying.

ALICK. All I can say is she has made a poor bargain.

MAGGIE (*the damned*). I wonder at you, father. He 's a very nice gentleman. I 'm sure I hope he has chosen wisely.

JAMES. Not him.

MAGGIE (*getting near her tragedy*). How can you say that when you don't know her? I expect she is full of charm.

ALICK. Charm? It 's the very word he used.

DAVID. Havering idiot.

ALICK. What *is* charm, exactly, Maggie?

MAGGIE. Oh, it 's—it 's a sort of bloom on a woman. If you have it, you don't need to have anything else; and if you don't have it, it doesn't much matter what else you have. Some women, the few, have charm for all; and most have charm for one. But some have charm for none.

(Somehow she has stopped knitting. Her men-folk are very depressed. JAMES brings his fist down on the table with a bang.)

JAMES *(shouting)*. I have a sister that has charm.

MAGGIE. No, James, you haven't.

JAMES *(rushing at her with the watch and chain)*. Ha'e, Maggie.

(She lets them lie in her lap.)

DAVID. Maggie, would you like a silk?

MAGGIE. What could I do with a silk? *(With a gust of passion.)* You might as well dress up a little brown hen.

(They wriggle miserably.)

JAMES *(stamping)*. Bring him here to me.

MAGGIE. Bring whom, James?

JAMES. David, I would be obliged if you wouldn't kick me beneath the table.

MAGGIE (*rising*). Let 's be practical; let 's go to our beds.

> (*This reminds them that they have a job on hand in which she is not to share.*)

DAVID (*slily*). I don't feel very sleepy yet.

ALICK. Nor me either.

JAMES. You 've just taken the very words out of my mouth.

DAVID (*with unusual politeness*). Good-night to you, Maggie.

MAGGIE (*fixing the three of them*). *All* of you unsleepy, when, as is well known, ten o'clock is your regular bed-time?

JAMES. Yes, it 's common knowledge that we go to our beds at ten. (*Chuckling.*) That 's what we 're counting on.

MAGGIE. Counting on?

DAVID. You stupid whelp.

JAMES. What have *I* done?

MAGGIE (*folding her arms*). There 's something up. You 've got to tell me, David.

DAVID (*who knows when he is beaten*).   Go out and watch, James.

MAGGIE.   Watch?

(JAMES *takes himself off, armed, as* MAGGIE *notices, with a stick.*)

DAVID (*in his alert business way*).   Maggie, there are burglars about.

MAGGIE.   Burglars? (*She sits rigid, but she is not the kind to scream.*)

DAVID.   We hadn't meant for to tell you till we nabbed them; but they 've been in this room twice of late. We sat up last night waiting for them, and we 're to sit up again to-night.

MAGGIE.   The silver plate.

DAVID.   It 's all safe as yet. That makes us think that they were either frightened away these other times, or that they are coming back for to make a clean sweep.

MAGGIE. How did you get to know about this?

DAVID. It was on Tuesday that the polissman called at the quarry with a very queer story. He had seen a man climbing out at this window at ten past two.

MAGGIE.   Did he chase him?

DAVID. It was so dark he lost sight of him at once.

ALICK. Tell her about the window.

DAVID. We 've found out that the catch of the window has been pushed back by slipping the blade of a knife between the woodwork.

MAGGIE. David.

ALICK. The polissman said he was carrying a little carpet bag.

MAGGIE. The silver plate *is* gone.

DAVID. No, no. We were thinking that very likely he has bunches of keys in the bag.

MAGGIE. Or weapons.

DAVID. As for that, we have some pretty stout weapons ourselves in the umbrella stand. So, if you 'll go to your bed, Maggie—

MAGGIE. Me? and my brothers in danger.

ALICK. There 's just one of them.

MAGGIE. The polissman just saw one.

DAVID (*licking his palms*). I would be very pleased if there were three of them.

MAGGIE. I watch with you. I would be very pleased if there were four of them.

DAVID. And they say she has no charm!

(JAMES *returns on tiptoe as if the burglars were beneath the table. He signs to every one to breathe no more, and then whispers his news.*)

JAMES. He's there. I had no sooner gone out than I saw him sliding down the garden wall, close to the rhubarbs.

ALICK. What's he like?

JAMES. He's an ugly customer. That's all I could see. There was a little carpet bag in his hand.

DAVID. That's him.

JAMES. He slunk into the rhodydendrons, and he's there now, watching the window.

DAVID. We have him. Out with the light.

(*The room is beautified by a chandelier fitted for three gas jets, but with the advance of progress one of these has been removed and the incandescent light put in its place. This alone is lit. ALICK climbs a chair, pulls a little chain, and the room is now but vaguely lit by the fire. It plays fitfully on four sparkling faces.*)

MAGGIE.   Do you think he saw you, James?

JAMES.   I couldn't say, but in any case I was too clever for him.   I looked up at the stars, and yawned loud at them as if I was tremendous sleepy.

(There is a long pause during which they are lurking in the shadows.   At last they hear some movement, and they steal like ghosts from the room.   We see DAVID *turning out the lobby light; then the door closes and an empty room awaits the intruder with a shudder of expectancy. The window opens and shuts as softly as if this were a mother peering in to see whether her baby is asleep.   Then the head of a man shows between the curtains.   The remainder of him follows.   He is carrying a little carpet bag.   He stands irresolute; what puzzles him evidently is that the Wylies should have retired to rest without lifting that piece of coal off the fire.   He opens the door and peeps into the lobby, listening to the wag-at-the-wall clock.   All seems serene, and he turns on the light.   We see him clearly*

now. He is JOHN SHAND, *age twenty-one, boots muddy, as an indignant carpet can testify. He wears a shabby topcoat and a cockerty bonnet; otherwise he is in the well-worn corduroys of a railway porter. His movements, at first stealthy, become almost homely as he feels that he is secure. He opens the bag and takes out a bunch of keys, a small paper parcel, and a black implement that may be a burglar's jemmy. This cool customer examines the fire and piles on more coals. With the keys he opens the door of the bookcase, selects two large volumes, and brings them to the table. He takes off his topcoat and opens his parcel, which we now see contains sheets of foolscap paper. His next action shows that the 'jemmy' is really a ruler. He knows where the pen and ink are kept. He pulls the fine chair nearer to the table, sits on it, and proceeds to write, occasionally dotting the carpet with ink as he stabs the air with his pen. He is so occupied that he does not see the door opening, and the*

Wylie family staring at him. They are armed with sticks.)

ALICK (*at last*). When you're ready, John Shand.

(JOHN *hints back, and then has the grace to rise, dogged and expressionless.*)

JAMES (*like a railway porter*). Ticket, please.

DAVID. You can't think of anything clever for to go for to say now, John.

MAGGIE. I hope you find that chair comfortable, young man.

JOHN. I have no complaint to make against the chair.

ALICK (*who is really distressed*). A native of the town. The disgrace to your family. I feel pity for the Shands this night.

JOHN (*glowering*). I'll thank you, Mr. Wylie, not to pity my family.

JAMES. Canny, canny.

MAGGIE (*that sense of justice again*). I think you should let the young man explain. It mayn't be so bad as we thought.

DAVID. Explain away, my billie.

JOHN. Only the uneducated would need an

explanation. I 'm a student, (*with a little passion*) and I 'm desperate for want of books. You have all I want here; no use to you but for display; well, I came here to study. I come twice weekly. (*Amazement of his hosts.*)

DAVID (*who is the first to recover*). By the window.

JOHN. Do you think a Shand would so far lower himself as to enter your door? Well, is it a case for the police?

JAMES. It is.

MAGGIE (*not so much out of the goodness of her heart as to patronise the Shands*). It seems to me it 's a case for us all to go to our beds and leave the young man to study; but not on that chair. (*And she wheels the chair away from him.*)

JOHN. Thank you, Miss Maggie, but I couldn't be beholden to you.

JAMES. My opinion is that he 's nobody, so out with him.

JOHN. Yes, out with me. And you 'll be cheered to hear I 'm likely to be a nobody for a long time to come.

DAVID (*who had been beginning to respect him*). Are you a poor scholar?

JOHN. On the contrary, I'm a brilliant scholar.

DAVID. It's siller, then?

JOHN (*glorified by experiences he has shared with many a gallant soul*). My first year at college I lived on a barrel of potatoes, and we had just a sofa-bed between two of us; when the one lay down the other had to get up. Do you think it was hardship? It was sublime. But this year I can't afford it. I'll have to stay on here, collecting the tickets of the illiterate, such as you, when I might be with Romulus and Remus among the stars.

JAMES (*summing up*). Havers.

DAVID (*in whose head some design is vaguely taking shape*). Whisht, James. I must say, young lad, I like your spirit. Now tell me, what's your professors' opinion of your future.

JOHN. They think me a young man of extraordinary promise.

DAVID. You have a name here for high moral character.

JOHN. And justly.

DAVID. Are you serious-minded?

JOHN. I never laughed in my life.

DAVID. Who do you sit under in Glasgow?

JOHN. Mr. Flemister of the Sauchiehall High.

DAVID. Are you a Sabbath-school teacher?

JOHN. I am.

DAVID. One more question. Are you promised?

JOHN. To a lady?

DAVID. Yes.

JOHN. I 've never given one of them a single word of encouragement. I 'm too much occupied thinking about my career.

DAVID. So. (*He reflects, and finally indicates by a jerk of the head that he wishes to talk with his father behind the door.*)

JAMES (*longingly*). Do you want me too?

(*But they go out without even answering him.*)

MAGGIE. I don't know what maggot they have in their heads, but sit down, young man, till they come back.

JOHN. My name 's Mr. Shand, and till I 'm

called that I decline to sit down again in this house.

MAGGIE. Then I'm thinking, young sir, you'll have a weary wait.

(*While he waits you can see how pinched his face is. He is little more than a boy, and he seldom has enough to eat.* DAVID *and* ALICK *return presently, looking as sly as if they had been discussing some move on the dambrod, as indeed they have.*)

DAVID (*suddenly become genial*). Sit down, Mr. Shand, and pull in your chair. You'll have a thimbleful of something to keep the cold out? (*Briskly.*) Glasses, Maggie.

(*She wonders, but gets glasses and decanter from the sideboard, which* JAMES *calls the chiffy.* DAVID *and* ALICK, *in the most friendly manner, also draw up to the table.*)

You're not a totaller, I hope?

JOHN (*guardedly*). I'm practically a totaller.

DAVID. So are we. How do you take it? Is there any hot water, Maggie?

JOHN. If I take it at all, and I haven't made up my mind yet, I 'll take it cold.

DAVID. You 'll take it hot, James?

JAMES (*also sitting at the table but completely befogged*). No, I—

DAVID (*decisively*). I think you 'll take it hot, James.

JAMES (*sulking*). I 'll take it hot.

DAVID. The kettle, Maggie.

> (JAMES *has evidently to take it hot so that they can get at the business now on hand, while* MAGGIE *goes kitchenward for the kettle.*)

ALICK. Now, David, quick, before she comes back.

DAVID. Mr. Shand, we have an offer to make you.

JOHN (*warningly*). No patronage.

ALICK. It 's strictly a business affair.

DAVID. Leave it to me, father. It 's this— (*But to his annoyance the suspicious* MAGGIE *has already returned with the kettle.*) Maggie, don't you see that you 're not wanted?

MAGGIE (*sitting down by the fire and resuming her knitting*). I do, David.

DAVID. I have a proposition to put before Mr. Shand, and women are out of place in business transactions.

(*The needles continue to click.*)

ALICK (*sighing*). We 'll have to let her bide, David.

DAVID (*sternly*). Woman. (*But even this does not budge her.*) Very well then, sit there, but don't interfere, mind. Mr. Shand, we 're willing, the three of us, to lay out £300 on your education if—

JOHN. Take care—

DAVID (*slowly, which is not his wont*). On condition that five years from now, Maggie Wylie, if still unmarried, can claim to marry you, should such be her wish; the thing to be perfectly open on her side, but you to be strictly tied down.

JAMES (*enlightened*). So, so.

DAVID (*resuming his smart manner*). Now, what have you to say? Decide.

JOHN (*after a pause*). I regret to say—

MAGGIE. It doesn't matter what he regrets to say, because I decide against it. And I think it was very ill-done of you to make any such proposal.

DAVID (*without looking at her*). Quiet, Maggie.

JOHN (*looking at her*). I must say, Miss Maggie, I don't see what reasons *you* can have for being so set against it.

MAGGIE. If you would grow a beard, Mr. Shand, the reasons wouldn't be quite so obvious.

JOHN. I'll never grow a beard.

MAGGIE. Then you're done for at the start.

ALICK. Come, come.

MAGGIE. Seeing I have refused the young man—

JOHN. Refused!

DAVID. That's no reason why we shouldn't have his friendly opinion. Your objections, Mr. Shand?

JOHN. Simply, it's a one-sided bargain. I admit I'm no catch at present; but what could a man of my abilities not soar to with three hundred pounds? Something far above what she could aspire to.

MAGGIE. Oh, indeed.

DAVID. The position is that without the three hundred you can't soar.

JOHN. You have me there.

MAGGIE. Yes, but—

ALICK. You see *you 're* safe-guarded, Maggie; you don't need to take him unless you like, but he has to take you.

JOHN. That 's an unfair arrangement also.

MAGGIE. I wouldn't dream of it without that condition.

JOHN. Then you *are* thinking of it?

MAGGIE. Poof.

DAVID. It 's a good arrangement for you, Mr. Shand. The chances are you 'll never have to go on with it, for in all probability she 'll marry soon.

JAMES. She 's tremendous run after.

JOHN. Even if that 's true, it 's just keeping me in reserve in case she misses doing better.

DAVID (*relieved*). That 's the situation in a nutshell.

JOHN. Another thing. Supposing I was to get fond of her?

ALICK (*wistfully*).   It's very likely.

JOHN.   Yes, and then suppose she was to give me the go-by?

DAVID.   You have to risk that.

JOHN.   Or take it the other way.   Supposing as I got to know her I *could not* endure her?

DAVID (*suavely*).   You have both to take risks.

JAMES (*less suavely*).   What you need, John Shand, is a clout on the head.

JOHN.   Three hundred pounds is no great sum.

DAVID.   You can take it or leave it.

ALICK.   No great sum for a student studying for the ministry!

JOHN.   Do you think that with that amount of money I would stop short at being a minister?

DAVID.   That's how I like to hear you speak. A young Scotsman of your ability let loose upon the world with £300, what could he not do?   It's almost appalling to think of; especially if he went among the English.

JOHN.   What do you think, Miss Maggie?

MAGGIE (*who is knitting*).   I have no thoughts on the subject either way.

JOHN (*after looking her over*).   What's her

age? She looks young, but they say it's the curls that does it.

DAVID (*rather happily*). She's one of those women who are eternally young.

JOHN. I can't take that for an answer.

DAVID. She's twenty-five.

JOHN. I'm just twenty-one.

JAMES. I read in a book that about four years' difference in the ages is the ideal thing. (*As usual he is disregarded.*)

DAVID. Well, Mr. Shand?

JOHN (*where is his mother!*) I'm willing if she's willing.

DAVID. Maggie?

MAGGIE. There can be no 'if' about it. It must be an offer.

JOHN. A Shand give a Wylie such a chance to humiliate him? Never.

MAGGIE. Then all is off.

DAVID. Come, come, Mr. Shand, it's just a form.

JOHN (*reluctantly*). Miss Maggie, will you?

MAGGIE (*doggedly*). Is it an offer?

JOHN (*dourly*). Yes.

MAGGIE (*rising*). Before I answer I want first to give you a chance of drawing back.

DAVID. Maggie.

MAGGIE (*bravely*). When they said that I have been run after they were misleading you. I 'm without charm; nobody has ever been after me.

JOHN. Oho!

ALICK. They will be yet.

JOHN (*the innocent*). It shows at least that you haven't been after them.

(*His hosts exchange a self-conscious glance.*)

MAGGIE. One thing more; David said I 'm twenty-five, I 'm twenty-six.

JOHN. Aha!

MAGGIE. Now be practical. Do you withdraw from the bargain, or do you not?

JOHN (*on reflection*). It 's a bargain.

MAGGIE. Then so be it.

DAVID (*hurriedly*). And that 's settled. Did you say you would take it hot, Mr. Shand?

JOHN. I think I 'll take it neat.

(*The others decide to take it hot, and there is some careful business here with the toddy ladles.*)

ALICK.   Here's to you, and your career.

JOHN.   Thank you. To you, Miss Maggie. Had we not better draw up a legal document? Lawyer Crosbie could do it on the quiet.

DAVID.   Should we do that, or should we just trust to one another's honour?

ALICK (*gallantly*).   Let Maggie decide.

MAGGIE.   I think we would better have a legal document.

DAVID.   We'll have it drawn up to-morrow. I was thinking the best way would be for to pay the money in five yearly instalments.

JOHN.   I was thinking, better bank the whole sum in my name at once.

ALICK.   I think David's plan's the best.

JOHN.   I think not. Of course if it's not convenient to you—

DAVID (*touched to the quick*).   It's perfectly convenient. What do you say, Maggie?

MAGGIE.   I agree with John.

DAVID (*with an odd feeling that* MAGGIE *is now on the other side*).   Very well.

JOHN.   Then as that's settled I think I'll be

stepping. (*He is putting his papers back in the bag.*)

ALICK (*politely*). If you would like to sit on at your books—

JOHN. As I can come at any orra time now I think I'll be stepping. (MAGGIE *helps him into his topcoat.*)

MAGGIE. Have you a muffler, John?

JOHN. I have. (*He gets it from his pocket.*)

MAGGIE. You had better put it twice round. (*She does this for him.*)

DAVID. Well good-night to you, Mr. Shand.

ALICK. And good luck.

JOHN. Thank you. The same to you. And I'll cry in at your office in the morning before the 6.20 is due.

DAVID. I'll have the document ready for you. (*There is the awkward pause that sometimes follows great events.*) I think, Maggie, you might see Mr. Shand to the door.

MAGGIE. Certainly. (JOHN *is going by the window.*) This way, John.

(*She takes him off by the more usual exit.*)

DAVID. He's a fine frank fellow; and you

saw how cleverly he got the better of me about banking the money. (*As the heads of the conspirators come gleefully together.*) I tell you, father, he has a grand business head.

ALICK. Lads, he's canny. He's cannier than any of us.

JAMES. Except maybe Maggie. He has no idea what a remarkable woman Maggie is.

ALICK. Best he shouldn't know. Men are nervous of remarkable women.

JAMES. She's a long time in coming back.

DAVID (*not quite comfortable*). It's a good sign. H'sh. What sort of a night is it, Maggie?

MAGGIE. It's a little blowy.

> (*She gets a large dust-cloth which is lying folded on a shelf, and proceeds to spread it over the fine chair. The men exchange self-conscious glances.*)

DAVID (*stretching himself*). Yes—well, well, oh yes. It's getting late. What is it with you, father?

ALICK. I'm ten forty-two.

JAMES. I'm ten forty.

DAVID. Ten forty-two.

(*They wind up their watches.*)

MAGGIE. It's high time we were bedded. (*She puts her hands on their shoulders lovingly, which is the very thing they have been trying to avoid.*) You're very kind to me.

DAVID. Havers.

ALICK. Havers.

JAMES (*but this does not matter*). Havers.

MAGGIE (*a little dolefully*). I'm a sort of sorry for the young man, David.

DAVID. Not at all. You'll be the making of him. (*She lifts the two volumes.*) Are you taking the books to your bed, Maggie?

MAGGIE. Yes. I don't want him to know things I don't know myself.

> (*She departs with the books; and* ALICK *and* DAVID, *the villains, now want to get away from each other.*)

ALICK. Yes—yes. Oh yes—ay, man—it is so—umpha. You'll lift the big coals off, David.

> (*He wanders away to his spring mattress.* DAVID *removes the coals.*)

JAMES (*who would like to sit down and have an argy-bargy*).   It 's a most romantical affair. (*But he gets no answer.*)   I wonder how it 'll turn out? (*No answer.*)   She 's queer, Maggie.   I wonder how some clever writer has never noticed how queer women are.   It 's my belief you could write a whole book about them.   (DAVID *remains obdurate.*)   It was very noble of her to tell him she 's twenty-six.   (*Muttering as he too wanders away.*)   But I thought she was twenty-seven.

(DAVID *turns out the light.*)

II

Six years have elapsed and John Shand's great hour has come. Perhaps his great hour really lies ahead of him, perhaps he had it six years ago; it often passes us by in the night with such a faint call that we don't even turn in our beds. But according to the trumpets this is John's great hour; it is the hour for which he has long been working with his coat off; and now the coat is on again (broadcloth but ill-fitting), for there is no more to do but await results. He is standing for Parliament, and this is election night.

As the scene discloses itself you get, so to speak, one of John Shand's posters in the face. Vote for Shand. Shand, Shand, Shand. Civil and Religious Liberty, Faith, Hope, Freedom. They are all fly-blown names for Shand. Have a placard about Shand, have a hundred placards about him, it is snowing Shand to-night in Glasgow; take the paste out of your eye, and you will see that we are in one of Shand's committee rooms. It has been a hairdresser's emporium, but Shand, Shand, Shand has swept through it like a *wind, leaving nothing but the fixtures; why shave, why have your head doused in those basins when you can be brushed and scraped and washed up for ever by simply voting for Shand?*

There are a few hard chairs for yelling Shand from, and then rushing away. There is an iron spiral staircase that once led to the ladies' hairdressing apartments, but now leads to more Shand, Shand, Shand. A glass door at the back opens on to the shop proper, screaming Civil and Religious Liberty, Shand, as it opens, and beyond is the street crammed with still more Shand pro and con. Men in every sort of garb rush in and out, up and down the stair, shouting the magic word. Then there is a lull, and down the stair comes Maggie Wylie, decidedly over-dressed in blue velvet and (let us get this over) less good-looking than ever. She raises her hands to heaven, she spins round like a little teetotum. To her from the street, suffering from a determination of the word Shand to the mouth, rush Alick and David. Alick is thinner (being older), David is stouter (being older), and they are both in tweeds and silk hats.

MAGGIE. David—have they—is he? quick, quick!

DAVID. There's no news yet, no news. It's terrible.

(*The teetotum revolves more quickly.*)

ALICK. For God's sake, Maggie, sit down.

MAGGIE. I can't, I can't.

DAVID. Hold her down.

(*They press her into a chair;* JAMES *darts in, stouter also. His necktie has gone; he will never again be able to attend a funeral in that hat.*)

JAMES (*wildly*). John Shand's the man for you. John Shand's the man for you. John Shand's the man for you.

DAVID (*clutching him*). Have you heard anything?

JAMES. Not a word.

ALICK. Look at her.

DAVID. Maggie (*he goes on his knees beside her, pressing her to him in affectionate anxiety*). It was mad of him to dare.

MAGGIE. It was grand of him.

ALICK (*moving about distraught*). Insane ambition.

MAGGIE. Glorious ambition.

DAVID. Maggie, Maggie, my lamb, best be prepared for the worst.

MAGGIE (*husky*). I am prepared.

ALICK. Six weary years has she waited for this night.

MAGGIE. Six brave years has John toiled for this night.

JAMES. And you could have had him, Maggie, at the end of five. The document says five.

MAGGIE. Do you think I grudge not being married to him yet? Was I to hamper him till the fight was won.

DAVID (*with wrinkled brows*). But if it 's lost?

> (*She can't answer.*)

ALICK (*starting*). What 's that?

> (*The three listen at the door; the shouting dies down.*)

DAVID. They 're terrible still; what can make them so still?

> (*JAMES spirits himself away. ALICK and DAVID blanch to hear MAGGIE speaking softly as if to JOHN.*)

MAGGIE. Did you say you had lost, John?

Of course you would lose the first time, dear John. Six years. Very well, we'll begin another six to-night. You'll win yet. (*Fiercely.*) Never give in, John, never give in!

(*The roar of the multitude breaks out again and comes rolling nearer.*)

DAVID. I think he's coming.

(JAMES *is fired into the room like a squeezed onion.*)

JAMES. He's coming!

(*They may go on speaking, but through the clang outside none could hear. The populace seem to be trying to take the committee room by assault. Out of the scrimmage a man emerges dishevelled and bursts into the room, closing the door behind him. It is* JOHN SHAND *in a five guinea suit, including the hat. There are other changes in him also, for he has been delving his way through loamy ground all those years. His right shoulder, which he used to raise to pound a path through the crowd, now remains permanently in that position. His mouth tends to close like a box. His eyes are tired, they need some one to pull the lids over them and send him to sleep for a week. But they are honest eyes still, and faithful, and could even light up his face at times with a smile, if the mouth would give a little help.*

JOHN (*clinging to a chair that he may not fly straight to heaven*). I'm in; I'm elected. Majority two hundred and forty-four; I'm John Shand, *M.P.*

(*The crowd have the news by this time and their roar breaks the door open. JAMES is off at once to tell them that he is to be Shand's brother-in-law. A teardrop clings to* ALICK'S *nose;* DAVID *hits out playfully at* JOHN, *and* JOHN *in an ecstasy returns the blow.*)

DAVID. Fling yourself at the door, father, and bar them out. Maggie, what keeps you so quiet now?

MAGGIE (*weak in her limbs*). You're sure you're in, John.

JOHN. Majority 244. I've beaten the baronet. I've done it, Maggie, and not a soul to help me; I've done it alone. (*His voice breaks; you*

could almost pick up the pieces.) I 'm as hoarse
as a crow, and I have to address the Cowcaddens
Club yet; David, pump some oxygen into me.

DAVID. Certainly, Mr. Shand. (*While he
does it,* MAGGIE *is seeing visions.*)

ALICK.   What are you doing, Maggie?

MAGGIE. This is the House of Commons, and
I 'm John, catching the Speaker's eye for the
first time. Do you see a queer little old wifie
sitting away up there in the Ladies' Gallery?
That 's me. Mr. Speaker, sir, I rise to make
my historic maiden speech. I am no orator,
sir; voice from Ladies' Gallery, 'Are you not,
John? you 'll soon let them see that'; cries of
'Silence, woman,' and general indignation. Mr.
Speaker, sir, I stand here diffidently with my
eyes on the Treasury Bench; voice from the
Ladies' Gallery, 'And you 'll soon have your
coat-tails on it, John'; loud cries of 'Remove
that little old wifie,' in which she is forcibly
ejected, and the honourable gentleman resumes
his seat in a torrent of admiring applause.

(ALICK *and* DAVID *waggle their proud
heads.*)

JOHN (*tolerantly*). Maggie, Maggie.

MAGGIE. You 're not angry with me, John?

JOHN. No, no.

MAGGIE. But you glowered.

JOHN. I was thinking of Sir Peregrine. Just because I beat him at the poll he took a shabby revenge; he congratulated me in French, a language I haven't taken the trouble to master.

MAGGIE (*becoming a little taller*). Would it help you, John, if you were to marry a woman that could speak French?

DAVID (*quickly*). Not at all.

MAGGIE (*gloriously*). Mon cher Jean, laissez-moi parler le français, voulez-vous un interprète?

JOHN. Hullo!

MAGGIE. Je suis la sœur française de mes deux frères écossais.

DAVID (*worshipping her*). She 's been learning French.

JOHN (*lightly*). Well done.

MAGGIE (*grandly*). They 're arriving.

ALICK. Who?

MAGGIE. Our guests. This is London, and

Mrs. John Shand is giving her first reception. (*Airily*). Have I told you, darling, who are coming to-night? There's that dear Sir Peregrine. (*To* ALICK.) Sir Peregrine, this *is* a pleasure. Avez-vous. . . . So sorry we beat you at the poll.

JOHN. I'm doubting the baronet would sit on you, Maggie.

MAGGIE. I've invited a lord to sit on the baronet. *Voilà!*

DAVID (*delighted*). You thing! You'll find the lords expensive.

MAGGIE. Just a little cheap lord. (JAMES *enters importantly.*) My dear Lord Cheap, this is kind of you.

> (JAMES *hopes that* MAGGIE'S *reason is not unbalanced.*)

DAVID (*who really ought to have had education*). How de doo, Cheap?

JAMES (*bewildered*). Maggie—

MAGGIE. Yes, do call me Maggie.

ALICK (*grinning*). She's practising her first party, James. The swells are at the door.

JAMES (*heavily*).   That's what I came to say. They *are* at the door.

JOHN.   Who?

JAMES.   The swells; a carriage and pair. (*He gives* JOHN *three cards.*)

JOHN.   'Mr. Tenterden.'

DAVID.   Him that was speaking for you?

JOHN.   The same.   He's a whip and an Honourable.   'Lady Sybil Tenterden.' (*Frowns.*)   Her!   She's his sister.

MAGGIE.   A married woman?

JOHN.   No.   'The Comtesse de la Brière.'

MAGGIE (*the scholar*).   She must be French.

JOHN.   Yes; I think she's some relation. She's a widow.

JAMES.   But what am I to say to them? ('*Mr. Shand's compliments, and he will be proud to receive them*' *is the very least that the Wylies expect.*)

JOHN (*who was evidently made for great ends*). Say I'm very busy, but if they care to wait I hope presently to give them a few minutes.

JAMES (*thunderstruck*).   Good God, Mr. Shand!

(*But it makes him* JOHN'S *more humble*

*servant than ever, and he departs with
the message.*)

JOHN (*not unaware of the sensation he has
created*). I 'll go up and let the crowd see me
from the window.

MAGGIE. But—but—what are we to do with
these ladies?

JOHN (*as he tramps upwards*). It 's your
reception, Maggie; this will prove you.

MAGGIE (*growing smaller*). Tell me what you
know about this Lady Sybil?

JOHN. The only thing I know about her is
that she thinks me vulgar.

MAGGIE. You?

JOHN. She has attended some of my meetings,
and I 'm told she said that.

MAGGIE. What could the woman mean?

JOHN. I wonder. When I come down I 'll
ask her.

(*With his departure* MAGGIE'S *nervousness
increases.*)

ALICK (*encouragingly*). In at them, Maggie,
with your French.

MAGGIE. It 's all slipping from me, father.

DAVID (*gloomily*). I'm sure to say 'for to come for to go.'

(*The new-comers glorify the room, and MAGGIE feels that they have lifted her up with the tongs and deposited her in one of the basins. They are far from intending to be rude; it is not their fault that thus do swans scatter the ducks. They do not know that they are guests of the family, they think merely that they are waiting with other strangers in a public room; they undulate enquiringly, and if MAGGIE could undulate in return she would have no cause for offence. But she suddenly realises that this is an art as yet denied her, and that though DAVID might buy her evening gowns as fine as theirs (and is at this moment probably deciding to do so), she would look better carrying them in her arms than on her person. She also feels that to emerge from wraps as they are doing is more difficult than to plank your money on the counter for them. The COMTESSE she could forgive, for she is old; but LADY*

SYBIL *is young and beautiful and comes lazily to rest like a stately ship of Tarsus.)*

COMTESSE (*smiling divinely, and speaking with such a pretty accent*). I hope one is not in the way. We were told we might wait.

MAGGIE (*bravely climbing out of the basin*). Certainly—I am sure—if you will be so—it is—

(*She knows that* DAVID *and her father are very sorry for her.*)

(*A high voice is heard orating outside.*)

SYBIL (*screwing her nose deliciously*). He is at it again, Auntie.

COMTESSE. Mon Dieu! (*Like one begging pardon of the universe.*) It is Mr. Tenterden, you understand, making one more of his delightful speeches to the crowd. *Would* you be so charming as to shut the door?

(*This to* DAVID *in such appeal that she is evidently making the petition of her life.* DAVID *saves her.*)

MAGGIE (*determined not to go under*). J'espère que vous — trouvez — cette — réunion — intéressante?

COMTESSE. Vous parlez français? Mais c'est

charmant! Voyons, causons un peu. Racontez-
moi tout de ce grand homme, toutes les choses
merveilleuses qu'il a faites.

MAGGIE.   I—I—Je connais—(*Alas!*)

COMTESSE (*naughtily*).   Forgive me, Made-
moiselle, I thought you spoke French.

SYBIL (*who knows that* DAVID *admires her
shoulders*).   How wicked of you, Auntie.   (*To*
MAGGIE.)   I assure you none of us can understand her when she gallops at that pace.

MAGGIE (*crushed*).   It doesn't matter.   I will
tell Mr. Shand that you are here.

SYBIL (*drawling*).   Please don't trouble him.
We are really only waiting till my brother re-
covers and can take us back to our hotel.

MAGGIE.   I 'll tell him.

(*She is glad to disappear up the stair.*)

COMTESSE.   The lady seems distressed.   Is
she a relation of Mr. Shand?

DAVID.   Not for to say a relation.   She 's my
sister.   Our name is Wylie.

(*But granite quarries are nothing to them.*)

COMTESSE.   How do you do.   You are the
committee man of Mr. Shand?

DAVID.   No, just friends.

COMTESSE (*gaily to the basins*).   Aha! I know you.   Next, please!   Sybil, do you weigh your-self, or are you asleep?

> (LADY SYBIL *has sunk indolently into a weighing-chair.*)

SYBIL. · Not quite, Auntie.

COMTESSE (*the mirror of la politesse*).   Tell me all about Mr. Shand.   Was it here that he—picked up the pin?

DAVID.   The pin?

COMTESSE.   As *I* have read, a self-made man always begins by picking up a pin.   After that, as the memoirs say, his rise was rapid.

> (DAVID, *however, is once more master of himself, and indeed has begun to tot up the cost of their garments.*)

DAVID.   It wasn't a pin he picked up, my lady; it was £300.

ALICK (*who feels that* JOHN's *greatness has been outside the conversation quite long enough*).   And his rise wasn't so rapid, just at first, David!

DAVID.   He had his fight.   His original in-tention was to become a minister; he's university-educated, you know; he 's not a working-man member.

ALICK (*with reverence*). He 's an M.A. But while he was a student he got a place in an iron cementer's business.

COMTESSE (*now far out of her depths*). Iron cementer?

DAVID. They scrape boilers.

COMTESSE. I see. The fun men have, Sybil!

DAVID (*with some solemnity*). There have been millions made in scraping boilers. They say, father, he went into business so as to be able to pay off the £300.

ALICK (*slily*). So I 've heard.

COMTESSE. Aha—it was a loan?

(DAVID *and* ALICK *are astride their great subject now.*)

DAVID. No, a gift—of a sort—from some well-wishers. But they wouldn't hear of his paying it off, father!

ALICK. Not them!

COMTESSE (*restraining an impulse to think of other things*). That was kind, charming.

ALICK (*with a look at* DAVID). Yes. Well,

my lady, he developed a perfect genius for the iron-cementing.

DAVID. But his ambition wasn't satisfied. Soon he had public life in his eye. As a heckler he was something fearsome; they had to seat him on the platform for to keep him quiet. Next they had to let him into the Chair. After that he did all the speaking; he cleared all roads before him like a fire-engine; and when this vacancy occurred, you could hardly say it did occur, so quickly did he step into it. My lady, there are few more impressive sights in the world than a Scotsman on the make.

COMTESSE. I can well believe it. And now he has said farewell to boilers?

DAVID (*impressively*). Not at all; the firm promised if he was elected for to make him their London manager at £800 a year.

COMTESSE. There is a strong man for you, Sybil; but I believe you *are* asleep.

SYBIL (*stirring herself*). Honestly I'm not. (*Sweetly to the others.*) But *would* you mind finding out whether my brother is drawing to a close?

(DAVID *goes out, leaving poor* ALICK *marooned. The* COMTESSE *is kind to him.*)

COMTESSE. Thank you very much. (*Which helps* ALICK *out.*) Don't you love a strong man, sleepy head?

SYBIL (*preening herself*). I never met one.

COMTESSE. Neither have I. But if you *did* meet one, would he wake you up?

SYBIL. I dare say he would find there were two of us.

COMTESSE (*considering her*). Yes, I think he would. Ever been in love, you cold thing?

SYBIL (*yawning*). I have never shot up in flame, Auntie.

COMTESSE. Think you could manage it?

SYBIL. If Mr. Right came along.

COMTESSE. As a girl of to-day it would be your duty to tame him.

SYBIL. As a girl of to-day I would try to do my duty.

COMTESSE. And if it turned out that *he* tamed you instead?

SYBIL. He would have to do that if he were *my* Mr. Right.

COMTESSE. And then?

SYBIL. Then, of course, I should adore him. Auntie, I think if I ever really love it will be like Mary Queen of Scots, who said of her Both-well that she could follow him round the world in her nighty.

COMTESSE. My petite!

SYBIL. I believe I mean it.

COMTESSE. Oh, it is quite my conception of your character. Do you know, I am rather sorry for this Mr. John Shand.

SYBIL (*opening her fine eyes*). Why? He is quite a boor, is he not?

COMTESSE. For that very reason. Because his great hour is already nearly sped. That wild bull manner that moves the multitude —they will laugh at it in your House of Commons.

SYBIL (*indifferent*). I suppose so.

COMTESSE. Yet if he had education—

SYBIL. Have we not been hearing how superbly he is educated?

COMTESSE. It is such as you or me that he needs to educate him now. *You* could do it almost too well.

SYBIL (*with that pretty stretch of neck*). I am not sufficiently interested. I retire in your favour. How would you begin?

COMTESSE. By asking him to drop in, about five, of course. By the way, I wonder is there a Mrs. Shand?

SYBIL. I have no idea. But they marry young.

COMTESSE. If there is not, there is probably a lady waiting for him, somewhere in a boiler.

SYBIL. I dare say.

(MAGGIE *descends*.)

MAGGIE. Mr. Shand will be down directly.

COMTESSE. Thank you. Your brother has been giving us such an interesting account of his career. I forget, Sybil, whether he said that he was married.

MAGGIE. No, he's not married; but he will be soon.

COMTESSE. Ah! (*She is merely making conversation*.) A friend of yours?

MAGGIE (*now a scorner of herself*). I don't think much of her.

COMTESSE. In that case, tell me all about her.

MAGGIE. There 's not much to tell. She 's common, and stupid. One of those who go in for self-culture; and then when the test comes they break down. (*With sinister enjoyment.*) She 'll be the ruin of him.

COMTESSE. But is not that sad! Figure to yourself how many men with greatness before them have been shipwrecked by marrying in the rank from which they sprang.

MAGGIE. I 've told her that.

COMTESSE. But she will not give him up?

MAGGIE. No.

SYBIL. Why should she if he cares for her? What is her name?

MAGGIE. It 's—Maggie.

COMTESSE (*still uninterested*). Well, I am afraid that Maggie is to do for John. (JOHN *comes down.*) Ah, our hero!

JOHN. Sorry I have kept you waiting. The Comtesse?

COMTESSE. And my niece Lady Sybil Tenterden. (SYBIL'S *head inclines on its stem.*) She is not really all my niece; I mean I am only half of her aunt. What a triumph, Mr. Shand!

JOHN. Oh, pretty fair, pretty fair. Your brother has just finished addressing the crowd, Lady Sybil.

SYBIL. Then we must not detain Mr. Shand, Auntie.

COMTESSE (*who unless her heart is touched thinks insincerity charming*). Only one word. I heard you speak last night. Sublime! Just the sort of impassioned eloquence that your House of Commons loves.

JOHN. It's very good of you to say so.

COMTESSE. But we must run. *Bon soir.*

(SYBIL *bows as to some one far away.*)

JOHN. Good-night, Lady Sybil. I hear you think I 'm vulgar.

(*Eyebrows are raised.*)

COMTESSE. My dear Mr. Shand, what absurd—

JOHN. I was told she said that after hearing me speak.

COMTESSE. Quite a mistake, I—

JOHN (*doggedly*). Is it not true?

SYBIL ('*waking up*'). You seem to know, Mr. Shand; and as you press me so unnecessarily—well, yes, that is how you struck me.

COMTESSE. My child!

SYBIL (*who is a little agitated*). He would have it.

JOHN (*perplexed*). What's the matter? I just wanted to know, because if it's true I must alter it.

COMTESSE. There, Sybil, see how he values your good opinion.

SYBIL (*her svelte figure giving like a fly-rod*). It is very nice of you to put it in that way, Mr. Shand. Forgive me.

JOHN. But I don't quite understand yet. Of course, it can't matter to me, Lady Sybil, what you think of me; what I mean is, that I mustn't be vulgar if it would be injurious to my career.

(*The fly-rod regains its rigidity.*)

SYBIL. I see. No, of course, I could not affect your career, Mr. Shand.

JOHN (*who quite understands that he is being*

challenged). That 's so, Lady Sybil, meaning no offence.

SYBIL (*who has a naughty little impediment in her voice when she is most alluring*). Of course not. And we are friends again?

JOHN. Certainly.

SYBIL. Then I hope you will come to see me in London as I present no terrors.

JOHN (*he is a man, is* JOHN). I 'll be very pleased.

SYBIL. Any afternoon about five.

JOHN. Much obliged. And you can teach me the things I don't know yet, if you 'll be so kind.

SYBIL (*the impediment becoming more assertive*). If you wish it, I shall do my best.

JOHN. Thank you, Lady Sybil. And who knows there may be one or two things I can teach you.

SYBIL (*it has now become an angel's hiccough*). Yes, we can help one another. Good-bye till then.

JOHN. Good-bye. Maggie, the ladies are going.

(*During this skirmish* MAGGIE *has stood apart. At the mention of her name they*

glance at one another. JOHN *escorts* SYBIL,
but the COMTESSE *turns back. She says:*
'Are you, then, *the* Maggie? (MAGGIE *nods
rather defiantly and the* COMTESSE *is distressed.*)
But if I had known I would not have said those
things. Please forgive an old woman.'

'It doesn't matter.'

'I—I dare say it will be all right. Made-
moiselle, if I were you I would not encourage
those *tête-à-têtes* with Lady Sybil. I am the
rude one, but she is the dangerous one; and
I am afraid his impudence has attracted her.
Bon voyage, Miss Maggie.'

'Good-bye—but I *can* speak French. Je parle
français. Isn't that right?'

'But, yes, it is excellent. (*Making things easy
for her.*) C'est très bien.'

'Je me suis embrouillée—la dernière fois.'

'Good! Shall I speak more slowly?'

'No, no. Non, non, faster, faster.'

'J'admire votre courage!'

'Je comprends chaque mot.'

'Parfait! Bravo!'

'Voilà!'

'Superbe!'

> (*The* COMTESSE *goes, applauding; and* MAGGIE *has a moment of elation, which however has passed before* JOHN *returns for his hat.*)

'Have you more speaking to do, John?'

> (*He is somehow in high good-humour.*)

'I must run across and address the Cow-caddens Club. (*He sprays his throat with a hand-spray.*) I wonder if I *am* vulgar, Maggie?'

'You are not, but *I* am.'

'Not that *I* can see.'

'Look how over-dressed I am, John! I knew it was too showy when I ordered it, and yet I could not resist the thing. But I will tone down, I will. What did you think of Lady Sybil?'

'That young woman had better be careful. She's a bit of a beson, Maggie.'

'She's beautiful, John.'

'She has a neat way of stretching herself. For playing with she would do as well as another.'

(MAGGIE *looks at him wistfully.*)

'You couldn't stay and have a talk for a few minutes?'

'If you want me, Maggie. The longer you keep them waiting, the more they think of you.'

'When are you to announce that we 're to be married, John?'

'I won't be long. You 've waited a year more than you need have done, so I think it 's your due I should hurry things now.'

'I think it 's noble of you.'

'Not at all, Maggie; the nobleness has been yours in waiting so patiently. And your brothers would insist on it at any rate. They 're watching me like cats with a mouse.'

'It 's so little I 've done to help.'

'Three hundred pounds.'

'I 'm getting a thousand per cent. for it.'

'And very pleased I am you should think so, Maggie.'

'Is it terrible hard to you, John?'

'It 's not hard at all. I can say truthfully, Maggie, that all, or nearly all, I 've seen of you in these six years has gone to increase my respect for you.'

'Respect!'

'And a bargain's a bargain.'

'If it wasn't that you're so glorious to me, John, I would let you off.'

(*There is a gleam in his eye, but he puts it out.*)

'In my opinion, Maggie, we'll be a very happy pair.'

(*She accepts this eagerly.*)

'We know each other so well, John, don't we?'

'I'm an extraordinary queer character, and I suppose nobody knows me well except myself; but I know you, Maggie, to the very roots of you.'

(*She magnanimously lets this remark alone.*)

'And it's not as if there was any other woman you—fancied more, John.'

'There's none whatever.'

'If there ever should be—oh, if there ever should be! Some woman with charm.'

'Maggie, you forget yourself. There couldn't be another woman once I was a married man.'

'One has heard of such things.'

'Not in Scotsmen, Maggie; not in Scotsmen.'

'I 've sometimes thought, John, that the difference between us and the English is that the Scotch are hard in all other respects but soft with women, and the English are hard with women but soft in all other respects.'

'You 've forgotten the grandest moral attribute of a Scotsman, Maggie, that he 'll do nothing which might damage his career.'

'Ah, but John, whatever you do, you do it so tremendously; and if you were to love, what a passion it would be.'

'There 's something in that, I suppose.'

'And then, what could I do? For the desire of my life now, John, is to help you to get everything you want, except just that I want you to have me, too.'

'We 'll get on fine, Maggie.'

'You 're just making the best of it. They say that love is sympathy, and if that 's so. mine must be a great love for you, for I see all you are feeling this night and bravely hiding;

I feel for you as if I was John Shand my-self.' (JOHN *sighs*.)

'I had best go to the meeting, Maggie.'

'Not yet. Can you look me in the face, John, and deny that there is surging within you a mighty desire to be free, to begin the new life untrammelled?'

'Leave such maggots alone, Maggie.'

'It's a shame of me not to give you up.'

'I would consider you a very foolish woman if you did.'

'If I were John Shand I would no more want to take Maggie Wylie with me through the beautiful door that has opened wide for you than I would want to take an old pair of shoon. Why don't you bang the door in my face, John?' (*A tremor runs through* JOHN.)

'A bargain's a bargain, Maggie.'

> (MAGGIE *moves about, an eerie figure, breaking into little cries. She flutters round him, threateningly.*)

'Say one word about wanting to get out of it, and 1'll put the lawyers on you.'

'Have I hinted at such a thing?'

'The document holds you hard and fast.'

'It does.'

(*She gloats miserably.*)

'The woman never rises with the man. I 'll drag you down, John.   I 'll drag you down.'

'Have no fear of that, I won't let you. I 'm too strong.'

'You 'll miss the prettiest thing in the world, and all owing to me.'

'What 's that?'

'Romance.'

'Poof.'

'All 's cold and grey without it, John. They that have had it have slipped in and out of heaven.'

'You 're exaggerating, Maggie.'

'You 've worked so hard, you 've had none of the fun that comes to most men long before they 're your age.'

'I never was one for fun. I cannot call to mind, Maggie, ever having laughed in my life.'

'You have no sense of humour.',

'Not a spark.'

'I 've sometimes thought that if you had, it might make you fonder of me. I think one needs a sense of humour to be fond of me.'

'I remember reading of some one that said it needed a surgical operation to get a joke into a Scotsman's head.'

'Yes, that 's been said.'

'What beats me, Maggie, is how you could insert a joke with an operation.'

(*He considers this and gives it up.*)

'That 's not the kind of fun I was thinking of. I mean fun with the lasses, John—gay, jolly, harmless fun. They could be impudent fashionable beauties now, stretching themselves to attract you, like that hiccoughing little devil, and running away from you, and crooking their fingers to you to run after them.'

(JOHN *draws a big breath.*)

'No, I never had that.'

'It 's every man's birthright, and you would have it now but for me.'

'I can do without, Maggie.'

'It 's like missing out all the Saturdays.'

'You feel sure, I suppose, that an older man wouldn't suit you better, Maggie?'

'I couldn't feel surer of anything. You 're just my ideal.'

'Yes, yes. Well, that 's as it should be.'

(*She threatens him again.*)

'David has the document. It 's carefully locked away.'

'He would naturally take good care of it.'

(*The pride of the Wylies deserts her.*)

'John, I make you a solemn promise that, in consideration of the circumstances of our marriage, if you should ever fall in love I 'll act differently from other wives.'

'There will be no occasion, Maggie.'

(*Her voice becomes tremulous.*)

'John, David doesn't have the document. He thinks he has, but I have it here.'

(*Somewhat heavily* JOHN *surveys the fatal paper.*)

'Well do I mind the look of it, Maggie. Yes, yes, that 's it. Umpha.'

'You don't ask why I 've brought it.'

'Why did you?'

'Because I thought I might perhaps have the courage and the womanliness to give it back to you. (JOHN *has a brief dream.*) Will you never hold it up against me in the future that I couldn't do that?'

'I promise you, Maggie, I never will.'

'To go back to the Pans and take up my old life there, when all these six years my eyes have been centred on this night! I 've been waiting for this night as long as you have been; and now to go back there, and wizen and dry up, when I might be married to John Shand!'

'And you will be, Maggie. You have my word.'

'Never—never—never. (*She tears up the document. He remains seated immovable, but the gleam returns to his eye. She rages first at herself and then at him.*) I 'm a fool, a fool, to let you go. I tell you, you 'll rue this day, for you need me, you 'll come to grief without me. There 's nobody can help you as I could have helped you. I'm essential to your career, and you're blind not to see it.'

'What's that, Maggie? In no circumstances would I allow any meddling with my career.'

'You would never have known I was meddling with it. But that's over. Don't be in too great a hurry to marry, John. Have your fling with the beautiful dolls first. Get the whiphand of the haughty ones, John. Give them their licks. Every time they hiccough let them have an extra slap in memory of me. And be sure to remember this, my man, that the one who marries you will find you out.'

'Find me out?'

'However careful a man is, his wife always finds out his failings.'

'I don't know, Maggie, to what failings you refer.

(The Cowcaddens Club has burst its walls, and is pouring this way to raise the new Member on its crest. The first wave hurls itself against the barber's shop with cries of

'Shand, Shand, Shand.' For a moment
JOHN *stems the torrent by planting his*
back against the door.)

You are acting under an impulse, Maggie, and I
can't take advantage of it. Think the matter
over, and we 'll speak about it in the morning.'

'No, I can't go through it again. It ends
to-night and now. Good luck, John.'

(She is immediately submerged in the sea
that surges through the door, bringing
much wreckage with it. In a moment the
place is so full that another cupful could
not find standing room. Some slippery
ones are squeezed upwards and remain aloft
as warnings. JOHN *has jumped on to the*
stair, and harangues the flood vainly like
another Canute. It is something about
freedom and noble minds, and, though
unheard, goes to all heads, including the
speaker's. By the time he is audible
sentiment has him for her own.)

'But, gentlemen, one may have too much
even of freedom. (*No, no.*) Yes, Mr. Adam-
son. One may want to be tied. (*Never,*

never.) I say yes, Willie Cameron; and I have found a young lady who I am proud to say is willing to be tied to me. I 'm to be married. (*Uproar.*) Her name 's Miss Wylie. (*Transport.*) Quiet; she 's here now. (*Frenzy.*) She was here! Where are you, Maggie?' (*A small voice*—'I 'm here.' *A hundred great voices*—'Where—where—where?' *The small voice*—'I 'm so little none of you can see me.')

> (*Three men, name of Wylie, buffet their way forward. Anon is heard the voice of* DAVID.)

'James, father, have you grip of her?'

'We 've got her.'

'Then hoist her up.'

> (*The queer little elated figure is raised aloft. With her fingers she can just touch the stars. Not unconscious of the nobility of his behaviour, the hero of the evening points an impressive finger at her.*)

'Gentlemen, the future Mrs. John Shand!' ('*Speech, speech.*') 'No, no, being a lady she can't make a speech, but—'

> (*The heroine of the evening surprises him.*)

'I can make a speech, and I will make a speech, and it's in two words, and they're these—(*holding out her arms to enfold all the members of the Cowcaddens Club*)—My Constituents!' (*Dementia.*)

III

A few minutes ago the Comtesse de la Brière, who has not recently been in England, was shown into the London home of the Shands. Though not sufficiently interested to express her surprise in words, she raised her eyebrows on finding herself in a charming room; she had presumed that the Shand scheme of decoration would be as impossible as themselves.

It is the little room behind the dining-room for which English architects have long been famous; 'Make something of this, and you will indeed be a clever one,' they seem to say to you as they unveil it. The Comtesse finds that John has undoubtedly made something of it. It is his 'study' (mon Dieu, the words these English use!) and there is nothing in it that offends; there is so much not in it too that might so easily have been there. It is not in the least ornate; there are no colours quarrelling with each other (unseen, unheard by the blissful occupant of the revolving chair); the Comtesse has not even the gentle satisfaction of noting a 'suite' in stained oak. Nature might have taken a share in the decorations, so restful are they to the eyes; it is the working room of a man of culture, probably lately down from Oxford; at a first meeting there is nothing in it that pretends to be what it is not. Our visitor is a little disappointed, but being fair-minded blows her absent host a kiss for disappointing her.

He has even, she observes with a twinkle, made something of the most difficult of his possessions, the little wife. For Maggie, who is here receiving her, has been quite creditably toned down. He has put her into a little grey frock that not only deals gently with her personal defects, but is in harmony with the room. Evidently, however, she has not 'risen' with him, for she is as stupid as ever; the Comtesse, who remembers having liked her the better of the two, could shake her for being so stupid. For instance, why is she not asserting herself in that other apartment?

The other apartment is really a correctly solemn din-ing-room, of which we have a glimpse through partly open folding-doors. At this moment it is harbouring Mr. Shand's ladies' committee, who sit with pens and foolscap round the large table, awaiting the advent of their leader. There are nobly wise ones and some foolish ones among them, for we are back in the strange days when it was considered 'unwomanly' for women

to have minds. *The Comtesse peeps at them with
curiosity, as they arrange their papers or are ushered
into the dining-room through a door which we cannot
see. To her frivolous ladyship they are a species of
wild fowl, and she is specially amused to find her
niece among them. She demands an explanation as
soon as the communicating doors close.*

'Tell me since when has my dear Sybil become
one of these ladies? It is not like her.'

(*MAGGIE is obviously not clever enough to
understand the woman question. Her eye
rests longingly on a half-finished stocking
as she innocently but densely replies:*)

'I think it was about the time that my
husband took up their cause.'

(*The COMTESSE has been hearing tales of
LADY SYBIL and the barbarian; and after
having the grace to hesitate, she speaks
with the directness for which she is famed
in Mayfair.*)

'Mrs. Shand, excuse me for saying that if
half of what I hear be true, your husband is

seeing that lady a great deal too often. (MAGGIE
*is expressionless; she reaches for her stocking,
whereat her guest loses patience.*) Oh, mon Dieu,
put that down; you can buy them at two
francs the pair. Mrs. Shand, why do not you
compel yourself to take an intelligent interest in
your husband's work?'

'I typewrite his speeches.'

'But do you know what they are about?'

'They are about various subjects.'

'Oh!'

> (*Did* MAGGIE *give her an unseen quizzical
> glance before demurely resuming the knit-
> ting? One is not certain, as* JOHN *has come
> in, and this obliterates her. A 'Scots-
> man on the make,' of whom* DAVID *has
> spoken reverently, is still to be read—in
> a somewhat better bound volume—in* JOHN
> SHAND'S *person; but it is as doggedly
> honest a face as ever; and he champions
> women, not for personal ends, but because
> his blessed days of poverty gave him a
> light upon their needs. His self-satisfac-
> tion, however, has increased, and he has*

*pleasantly forgotten some things. For
instance, he can now call out 'Porter' at
railway stations without dropping his hands
for the barrow.* MAGGIE *introduces the*
COMTESSE, *and he is still undaunted.*)

'I remember you well—at Glasgow.'

'It must be quite two years ago, Mr. Shand.'

(JOHN *has no objection to showing that he
has had a classical education.*)

'*Tempus fugit*, Comtesse.'

'I have not been much in this country since
then, and I return to find you a coming
man.'

(*Fortunately his learning is tempered with
modesty.*)

'Oh, I don't know, I don't know.'

'The Ladies' Champion.'

(*His modesty is tempered with a respect
for truth.*)

'Well, well.'

'And you are about, as I understand, to introduce a bill to give women an equal right
with men to grow beards (*which is all she knows
about it.* JOHN *takes the remark literally.*)

'There's nothing about beards in it, Comtesse. (*She gives him time to cogitate, and is pleased to note that there is no result.*)   Have you typed my speech, Maggie?'

'Yes; twenty-six pages.' (*She produces it from a drawer.*)

(*Perhaps* JOHN *wishes to impress the visitor.*)

'I'm to give the ladies' committee a general idea of it. Just see, Maggie, if I know the peroration. "In conclusion, Mr. Speaker, these are the reasonable demands of every intelligent English-woman"—I had better say British woman—"and I am proud to nail them to my flag"'—

(*The visitor is properly impressed.*)

'Oho! defies his leaders!'

' "So long as I can do so without embarrass-ing the Government." '

'Ah, ah, Mr. Shand!'

' "I call upon the Front Bench, sir, loyally but firmly" '—

'Firm again!'

'. . . . "either to accept my Bill, or to pro-mise *without delay* to bring in one of their

own; and if they decline to do so I solemnly
warn them that though I will not press the
matter to a division just now" '—

'Ahem!'

' "I will bring it forward again in the near
future." And now, Comtesse, *you* know that
I 'm not going to divide—and not another soul
knows it.'

'I am indeed flattered by your confidence.'

'I 've only told you because I don't care who
knows now.'

'Oh!'

(*Somehow* MAGGIE *seems to be dissatisfied.*)

'But why is that, John?'

'I daren't keep the Government in doubt
any longer about what I mean to do. I 'll show
the whips the speech privately to-night.'

(*But still* MAGGIE *wants to know.*) 'But not
to go to a division is hedging, isn't it? Is that
strong?'

'To make the speech at all, Maggie, is stronger
than most would dare. They would *do* for me
if I went to a division.'

'Bark but not bite?'

'Now, now, Maggie, you 're out of your depth.'

'I suppose that 's it.'

(*The* COMTESSE *remains in the shallows.*)

'But what will the ladies say, Mr. Shand?'

'They won't like it, Comtesse, but they 've got to lump it.'

(*Here the* MAID *appears with a card for* MAGGIE, *who considers it quietly.*)

'Any one of importance?'

'No.'

'Then I 'm ready, Maggie.'

(*This is evidently an intimation that she is to open the folding-doors, and he makes an effective entrance into the dining-room, his thumb in his waistcoat.   There is a delicious clapping of hands from the committee, and the door closes.   Not till then does* MAGGIE, *who has grown thoughtful, tell her maid to admit the visitor.*)

'Another lady, Mrs. Shand?'

'The card says "Mr. Charles Venables." '

(*The* COMTESSE *is really interested at last.*)

'Charles Venables! Do *you* know him?'

'I think I call to mind meeting one of that name at the Foreign Office party.'

'One of that name! He who is a Minister of your Cabinet. But as you know him so little why should he call on you?'

'I wonder.'

> (MAGGIE's *glance wanders to the drawer in which she has replaced* JOHN's *speech*.)

'Well, well, I shall take care of you, petite.'

'Do *you* know him?'

'Do I know him! The last time I saw him he asked me to—to—hem!—ma chérie, it was thirty years ago.'

'Thirty years!'

'I was a pretty woman then. I dare say I shall detest him now; but if I find I do not—let us have a little plot—I shall drop this book; and then perhaps you will be so charming as—as not to be here for a little while?'

> (MR. VENABLES, *who enters, is such a courtly seigneur that he seems to bring the eighteenth century with him; you feel that his sedan chair is at the door. He stoops over* MAGGIE's *plebeian hand.*)

'I hope you will pardon my calling, Mrs. Shand; we had such a pleasant talk the other evening.'

(MAGGIE, *of course, is at once deceived by his gracious manner.*)

'I think it's kind of you.   Do you know each other?   The Comtesse de la Brière.'

(*He repeats the name with some emotion, and the* COMTESSE *half mischievously, half sadly, holds a hand before her face.*)

'Comtesse.'

'Thirty years, Mr. Venables.'

(*He gallantly removes the hand that screens her face.*)

'It does not seem so much.'

(*She gives him a similar scrutiny.*)

'Mon Dieu, it seems all that.'

(*They smile rather ruefully.* MAGGIE *like a kind hostess relieves the tension.*)

'The Comtesse has taken a cottage in Surrey for the summer.'

'I am overjoyed.'

'No, Charles, you are not.   You no longer

care. Fickle one! And it is only thirty years.'

(He sinks into a chair beside her.)

'Those heavenly evenings, Comtesse, on the Bosphorus.'

'I refuse to talk of them. I hate you.'

(But she drops the book, and MAGGIE *fades from the room. It is not a very clever departure, and the old diplomatist smiles. Then he sighs a beautiful sigh, for he does all things beautifully.)*

'It is moonlight, Comtesse, on the Golden Horn.'

'Who are those two young things in a caïque?'

'Is he the brave Leander, Comtesse, and is she Hero of the Lamp?'

'No, she is the foolish wife of the French Ambassador, and he is a good-for-nothing British attaché trying to get her husband's secrets out of her.'

'Is it possible! They part at a certain garden gate.'

'Oh, Charles, Charles!'

'But you promised to come back; I waited

there till dawn. Blanche, if you *had* come back—'

'How is Mrs. Venables?'

'She is rather poorly. *I* think it 's gout.'

'And you?'

'I creak a little in the mornings.'

'So do I. There is such a good man at Wiesbaden.'

'The Homburg fellow is better. The way he patched me up last summer—Oh, Lord, Lord!'

'Yes, Charles, the game is up; we are two old fogies. (*They groan in unison; then she raps him sharply on the knuckles.*) Tell me, sir, what are you doing here?'

'Merely a friendly call.'

'I do not believe it.'

'The same woman; the old delightful candour.'

'The same man; the old fibs. (*She sees that the door is asking a question.*) Yes, come, Mrs. Shand, I have had quite enough of him; I warn you he is here for some crafty purpose.'

MAGGIE (*drawing back timidly*). Surely not?

VENABLES. Really, Comtesse, you make con-

versation difficult. To show that my intentions
are innocent, Mrs. Shand, I propose that you
choose the subject.

MAGGIE (*relieved*). There, Comtesse.

VENABLES. I hope your husband is well?

MAGGIE. Yes, thank you. (*With a happy
thought.*) I decide that we talk about him.

VENABLES. If you wish it.

COMTESSE. Be careful; *he* has chosen the
subject.

MAGGIE. *I* chose it, didn't I?

VENABLES. You know you did.

MAGGIE (*appealingly*). You admire John?

VENABLES. Very much. But he puzzles me
a little. You Scots, Mrs. Shand, are such a
mixture of the practical and the emotional that
you escape out of an Englishman's hand like a
trout.

MAGGIE (*open-eyed*). Do we?

VENABLES. Well, not you, but your husband.
I have known few men make a worse beginning
in the House. He had the most atrocious bow-
wow public park manner—

COMTESSE. I remember that manner!

MAGGIE.   No, he hadn't.

VENABLES (*soothingly*).   At first.   But by his second session he had shed all that, and he is now a pleasure to listen to.   By the way, Comtesse, have you found any dark intention in that?

COMTESSE.   You wanted to know whether he talks over these matters with his wife; and she has told you that he does not.

MAGGIE (*indignantly*).   I haven't said a word about it, have I?

VENABLES.   Not a word.   Then, again, I admire him for his impromptu speeches.

MAGGIE.   What is impromptu?

VENABLES.   Unprepared.   They have contained some grave blunders, not so much of judgment as of taste—

MAGGIE (*hotly*).   *I* don't think so.

VENABLES.   Pardon me.   But he has righted himself subsequently in the neatest way.   I have always found that the man whose second thoughts are good is worth watching.   Well, Comtesse, I see you have something to say.

COMTESSE.   You are wondering whether she can tell you who gives him his second thoughts.

MAGGIE. Gives them to John? I would like to see anybody try to give thoughts to John.

VENABLES. Quite so.

COMTESSE. Is there anything more that has roused your admiration, Charles?

VENABLES (*purring*). Let me see. Yes, we are all much edified by his humour.

COMTESSE (*surprised indeed*). His humour? That man!

MAGGIE (*with hauteur*). Why not?

VENABLES. I assure you, Comtesse, some of the neat things in his speeches convulse the house. A word has even been coined for them —Shandisms.

COMTESSE (*slowly recovering from a blow*). Humour!

VENABLES. In conversation, I admit, he strikes one as being—ah—somewhat lacking in humour.

COMTESSE (*pouncing*). You are wondering who supplies his speeches with the humour.

MAGGIE. Supplies John?

VENABLES. Now that you mention it, some

of his Shandisms do have a curiously feminine quality.

COMTESSE. You have thought it might be a woman.

VENABLES. Really, Comtesse—

COMTESSE. I see it all. Charles, you thought it might be the wife!

VENABLES (*flinging up his hands*). I own up.

MAGGIE (*bewildered*). Me?

VENABLES. Forgive me, I see I was wrong.

MAGGIE (*alarmed*). Have I been doing John any harm?

VENABLES. On the contrary, I am relieved to know that there are no hairpins in his speeches. If he is at home, Mrs. Shand, may I see him? I am going to be rather charming to him.

MAGGIE (*drawn in two directions*). Yes, he is— oh yes—but—

VENABLES. That is to say, Comtesse, if he proves himself the man I believe him to be.

(*This arrests* MAGGIE *almost as she has reached the dining-room door.*)

MAGGIE (*hesitating*). He is very busy just now.

VENABLES (*smiling*). I think he will see me.

MAGGIE. Is it something about his speech?

VENABLES (*the smile hardening*). Well, yes, it is.

MAGGIE. Then I dare say I could tell you what you want to know without troubling him, as I 've been typing it.

VENABLES (*with a sigh*). I don't acquire information in that way.

COMTESSE. I trust not.

MAGGIE. There's no secret about it. He is to show it to the Whips to-night.

VENABLES (*sharply*). You are sure of that?

COMTESSE. It is quite true, Charles. I heard him say so; and indeed he repeated what he called the 'peroration' before me.

MAGGIE. I know it by heart. (*She plays a bold game.*) 'These are the demands of all intelligent British women, and I am proud to nail them to my flag'—

COMTESSE. The very words, Mrs. Shand.

MAGGIE (*looking at her imploringly*). 'And I don't care how they may embarrass the Government.' (*The* COMTESSE *is bereft of speech, so suddenly has she been introduced to the*

real MAGGIE SHAND.)   'If the right honourable
gentleman will give us his pledge to introduce a
similar bill this session I will willingly withdraw
mine; but otherwise I solemnly warn him that
I will press the matter now to a division.'

> (*She turns her face from the great man;
> she has gone white.*)

VENABLES (*after a pause*).   Capital.

> (*The blood returns to* MAGGIE'S *heart.*)

COMTESSE (*who is beginning to enjoy herself
very much*).   Then you are pleased to know
that he means to, as you say, go to a division?

VENABLES.   Delighted.   The courage of it
will be the making of him.

COMTESSE.   I see.

VENABLES.   Had he been to hedge we should
have known that he was a pasteboard knight
and have disregarded him.

COMTESSE.   I see.

> (*She desires to catch the eye of* MAGGIE,
> but it is carefully turned from her.*)

VENABLES.   Mrs. Shand, let us have him in
at once.

COMTESSE.   Yes, yes, indeed.

(MAGGIE'S *anxiety returns, but she has to call* JOHN *in.*)

JOHN (*impressed*).   Mr. Venables! This is an honour.

VENABLES.   How are you, Shand?

JOHN.   Sit down, sit down. (*Becoming himself again.*) I can guess what you have come about.

VENABLES.   Ah, you Scotsmen.

JOHN.   Of course I know I 'm harassing the Government a good deal—

VENABLES (*blandly*).   Not at all, Shand. The Government are very pleased.

JOHN.   You don't expect me to believe that.

VENABLES.   I called here to give you the proof of it. You may know that we are to have a big meeting at Leeds on the 24th, when two Ministers are to speak. There is room for a third speaker, and I am authorised to offer that place to you.

JOHN.   To me!

VENABLES.   Yes.

JOHN (*swelling*).   It would be—the Government taking me up.

VENABLES.   Don't make too much of it; it

would be an acknowledgment that they look upon you as one of their likely young men.

MAGGIE.   John!

JOHN (*not found wanting in a trying hour*). It's a bribe.   You are offering me this on condition that I don't make my speech.   How can you think so meanly of me as to believe that I would play the women's cause false for the sake of my own advancement.   I refuse your bribe.

VENABLES (*liking him for the first time*). Good.   But you are wrong.   There are no conditions, and we want you to make your speech. Now do you accept?

JOHN (*still suspicious*).   If you make me the same offer after you have read it.   I insist on your reading it first.

VENABLES (*sighing*).   By all means.

(MAGGIE *is in an agony as she sees* JOHN *hand the speech to his leader.   On the other hand, the* COMTESSE *thrills.*)

But I assure you we look on the speech as a small matter.   The important thing is your intention of going to a division; and we agree to that also.

JOHN (*losing his head*).   What's that?

VENABLES.   Yes, we agree.

JOHN.   But—but—why, you have been threatening to excommunicate me if I dared.

VENABLES.   All done to test you, Shand.

JOHN.   To test me?

VENABLES.   We know that a division on your Bill can have no serious significance; we shall see to that.   And so the test was to be whether you had the pluck to divide the House.   Had you been intending to talk big in this speech, and then hedge, through fear of the Government, they would have had no further use for you.

JOHN (*heavily*).   I understand.   (*But there is one thing he cannot understand, which is, why* VENABLES *should be so sure that he is not to hedge.*)

VENABLES (*turning over the pages carelessly*).   Any of your good things in this, Shand?

JOHN (*whose one desire is to get the pages back*).   No, I—no—it isn't necessary you should read it now.

VENABLES (*from politeness only*).   Merely for my own pleasure.   I shall look through it this evening.   (*He rolls up the speech to put it in his pocket.* JOHN *turns despairingly to* MAGGIE, *though well aware that no help can come from her.*)

MAGGIE. That's the only copy there is, John. (*To* VENABLES.) Let me make a fresh one, and send it to you in an hour or two.

VENABLES (*good-naturedly*). I could not put you to that trouble, Mrs. Shand. I will take good care of it.

MAGGIE. If anything were to happen to you on the way home, wouldn't whatever is in your pocket be considered to be the property of your heirs?

VENABLES (*laughing*). Now there is fore-thought! Shand, I think that after that—! (*He returns the speech to* JOHN, *whose hand swallows it greedily.*) She is Scotch too, Comtesse.

COMTESSE (*delighted*). Yes, she is Scotch too.

VENABLES. Though the only persons likely to do for me in the street, Shand, are your ladies' committee. Ever since they took the horse out of my brougham, I can scent them a mile away.

COMTESSE. A mile? Charles, peep in there.

(*He softly turns the handle of the dining-*

*room door, and realises that his scent is
not so good as he had thought it. He bids
his hostess and the* COMTESSE *good-bye in a
burlesque whisper and tiptoes off to safer
places.* JOHN *having gone out with him,*
MAGGIE *can no longer avoid the* COMTESSE'S
*reproachful eye. That much injured lady
advances upon her with accusing finger.*)

'So, madam!'

(MAGGIE *is prepared for her.*)

'I don't know what you mean.'

'Yes, you do. I mean that there *is* some
one who "helps" our Mr. Shand.'

'There 's not.'

'And it *is* a woman, and it 's you.'

'I help in the little things.'

'The little things! You are the Pin he
picked up and that is to make his fortune. And
now what I want to know is whether your
John is aware that you help at all.'

(JOHN *returns, and at once provides the answer.*)

'Maggie, Comtesse, I 've done it again!'

'I 'm so glad, John.'

(*The* COMTESSE *is in an ecstasy.*)

'And all because you were not to hedge, Mr. Shand.'

(*His appeal to her with the wistfulness of a schoolboy makes him rather attractive.*)

'You won't tell on me, Comtesse! (*He thinks it out.*) They had just guessed I would be firm because they know I 'm a strong man. You little saw, Maggie, what a good turn you were doing me when you said you wanted to make another copy of the speech.'

(*She is dense.*)

'How, John?'

'Because now I can alter the end.'

(*She is enlightened.*)

'So you can!'

'Here 's another lucky thing, Maggie: I hadn't told the ladies' committee that I was to hedge, and so they need never know. Comtesse, I tell you there 's a little cherub who sits up aloft and looks after the career of John Shand.'

(*The* COMTESSE *looks not aloft but toward the chair at present occupied by* MAGGIE.)

'Where does she sit, Mr. Shand?'

(*He knows that women are not well read.*)

'It 's just a figure of speech.'

(*He returns airily to his committee room;
and now again you may hear the click of
MAGGIE's needles. They no longer annoy
the COMTESSE; she is setting them to music.*)

'It is not down here she sits, Mrs. Shand,
knitting a stocking.'

'No, it isn't.'

'And when I came in I gave him credit for
everything; even for the prettiness of the room !'

'He has beautiful taste.'

'Good-bye, Scotchy.'

'Good-bye, Comtesse, and thank you for
coming.'

'Good-bye—Miss Pin.'

(MAGGIE *rings genteelly*.)

'Good-bye.'

(*The* COMTESSE *is now lost in admiration
of her.*)

'You divine little wife. He can't be worthy
of it, no man could be worthy of it. Why do
you do it ?'

(MAGGIE *shivers a little*.)

'He loves to think he does it all himself;

that's the way of men. I'm six years older than he is. I'm plain, and I have no charm. l shouldn't have let him marry me. I'm trying to make up for it.'

> (*The* COMTESSE *kisses her and goes away.* MAGGIE, *somewhat foolishly, resumes her knitting.*)

Some days later this same room is listening—with the same inattention—to the outpouring of JOHN SHAND'S *love for the lady of the hiccoughs. We arrive—by arrangement—rather late; and thus we miss some of the most delightful of the pangs.*

One can see that these two are playing no game, or, if they are, that they little know it. The wonders of the world (so strange are the instruments chosen by Love) have been revealed to JOHN *in hiccoughs; he shakes in* SYBIL'S *presence; never were more swimming eyes; he who has been of a wooden face till now, with ways to match, has gone on flame like a piece of paper; emotion is in flood in him. We may be almost fond of* JOHN *for being so worshipful of love.   Much has come to him that we had almost despaired of his acquiring, including nearly all the divine attributes except that sense of humour. The beautiful* SYBIL *has always possessed but little of it also, and what she had has been struck from her by Cupid's flail. Naked of the saving grace, they face each other in awful rapture.)*

'In a room, Sybil, I go to you as a cold man to a fire.   You fill me like a peal of bells in an empty house.'

(She is being brutally treated by the dear impediment, for which hiccough is such an inadequate name that even to spell it is an abomination though a sign of ability. How to describe a sound that is noiseless?   Let us put it thus, that when SYBIL *wants to say something very much there are little obstacles in her way; she falters, falls perhaps once, and then is over, the while her appealing orbs beg you not to be angry*

*with her. We may express those sweet
pauses in precious dots, which some clever
person can afterwards string together and
make a pearl necklace of them.*)

'I should not . . . let you say it, . . . but
. . . you . . . say it so beautifully.'

'You must have guessed.'

'I dreamed . . . I feared . . . but you were
. . . Scotch, and I didn't know what to think.'

'Do you know what first attracted me to
you, Sybil? It was your insolence. I thought,
"I'll break her insolence for her."'

'And I thought . . . "I'll break his
str . . . ength!"'

'And now your cooing voice plays round
me; the softness of you, Sybil, in your pretty
clothes makes me think of young birds. (*The
impediment is now insurmountable; she has to
swim for it, she swims toward him.*) It is you
who inspire my work.'

(*He thrills to find that she can be touched
without breaking.*)

'I am so glad . . . so proud . . .'

'And others know it, Sybil, as well as I.

Only yesterday the Comtesse said to me, "No man could get on so fast unaided. *Cherchez la femme*, Mr. Shand." '

'Auntie said that!'

'I said "Find her yourself, Comtesse." '

'And she?'

'She said "I have found her," and I said in my blunt way, "You mean Lady Sybil," and she went away laughing.'

'Laughing?'

'I seem to amuse the woman.'

(SYBIL *grows sad.*)

'If Mrs. Shand— It is so cruel to her. Whom did you say she had gone to the station to meet?'

'Her father and brothers.'

'It is so cruel to them. We must think no more of this. It is mad . . . ness.'

'It's fate. Sybil, let us declare our love openly.'

'You can't ask that, now in the first moment that you tell me of it.'

'The one thing I won't do even for you is to live a life of underhand.'

'The . . . blow to her.'

'Yes.   But at least she has always known that I never loved her.'

'It is asking me to give . . . up everything, every one, for you.'

'It 's too much.'

(JOHN *is humble at last.*)

'To a woman who truly loves, even that is not too much.   Oh! it is not I who matter—it is you.'

'My dear, my dear.'

'So gladly would I do it to save you; but, oh, if it were to bring you down!'

'Nothing can keep me down if I have you to help me.'

'I am dazed, John, I . . .'

'My love, my love.'

'I . . . oh . . . here . . .'

'Be brave, Sybil, be brave.'

'. . . . .'

(*In this bewilderment of pearls she melts into his arms.*   MAGGIE *happens to open the door just then; but neither fond heart hears her.*)

'I can't walk along the streets, Sybil, without looking in all the shop windows for what I think would become you best. (*As awkwardly as though his heart still beat against corduroy, he takes from his pocket a pendant and its chain. He is shy, and she drops pearls over the beauty of the ruby which is its only stone.*) It is a drop of my blood, Sybil.'

> (*Her lovely neck is outstretched, and he puts the chain round it. MAGGIE withdraws as silently as she had come; but perhaps the door whispered 'd—n,' or (humorously) 'd .. n' as it closed, for SYBIL wakes out of Paradise.*)

'I thought— Did the door shut?'

'It was shut already.'

> (*Perhaps it is only that SYBIL is bewildered to find herself once again in a world that has doors.*)

'It seemed to me—'

'There was nothing. But I think I hear voices; they may have arrived.'

> (*Some pretty instinct makes SYBIL go farther from him. MAGGIE kindly gives*

*her time for this by speaking before open-
ing the door.)*

'That will do perfectly, David. The maid
knows where to put them. (*She comes in.*)
They 've come, John; they *would* help with the
luggage. (JOHN *goes out.* MAGGIE *is agreeably
surprised to find a visitor.*) How do you do,
Lady Sybil? This is nice of you.'

'I was so sorry not to find you in, Mrs.
Shand.'

> *(The impediment has run away. It is only*
> *for those who love it.)*

'Thank you. You 'll sit down?'

'I think not; your relatives—'

'They will be so proud to see that you are
my friend.'

> *(If* MAGGIE *were less simple her guest would*
> *feel more comfortable. She tries to make*
> *conversation.)*

'It is their first visit to London?'

> *(Instead of relieving her anxiety on this*
> *point,* MAGGIE *has a long look at the gorgeous*
> *armful.)*

'I 'm glad you are so beautiful, Lady Sybil.'

*(The beautiful one is somehow not flat-
tered. She pursues her investigations with
growing uneasiness.)*

'One of them is married now, isn't he?
(Still there is no answer; MAGGIE *continues
looking at her, and shivers slightly.)* Have they
travelled from Scotland to-day? Mrs. Shand,
why do you look at me so? The door did
open! (*MAGGIE* nods.) What are you to
do?'

'That would be telling. Sit down, my pretty.'

(As SYBIL *subsides into what the Wylies
with one glance would call the best chair,*
MAGGIE'S *men-folk are brought in by* JOHN,
*all carrying silk hats and looking very active
after their long rest in the train. They
are gazing about them. They would like
this lady, they would like* JOHN, *they would
even like* MAGGIE *to go away for a little
and leave them to examine the room. Is
that linen on the walls, for instance, or
just paper? Is the carpet as thick as it
feels, or is there brown paper beneath it?
Had* MAGGIE *got anything off that book-*

case on account of the worm-holes? DAVID *even discovers that we were simpletons when we said there was nothing in the room that pretended to be what it was not. He taps the marble mantelpiece, and is favourably impressed by the tinny sound.*)

DAVID. Very fine imitation. It's a capital house, Maggie.

MAGGIE. I'm so glad you like it. Do you know one another? This is my father and my brothers, Lady Sybil.

(*The lovely form inclines toward them.* ALICK *and* JOHN *remain firm on their legs, but* JAMES *totters.*)

JAMES. A ladyship! Well done, Maggie.

ALICK (*sharply*). James! I remember you, my lady.

MAGGIE. Sit down, father. This is the study.

(JAMES *wanders round it inquisitively until called to order.*)

SYBIL. You must be tired after your long journey.

DAVID (*drawing the portraits of himself and partners in one lightning sketch*). Tired, your ladyship? We sat on cushioned seats the whole way.

JAMES (*looking about him for the chair you sit on*). Every seat in this room is cushioned.

MAGGIE. You may say all my life is cushioned now, James, by this dear man of mine.

> (*She gives* JOHN'S *shoulder a loving pressure, which* SYBIL *feels is a telegraphic communication to herself in a cypher that she cannot read.* ALICK *and the* BROTHERS *bask in the evidence of* MAGGIE'S *happiness.*)

JOHN (*uncomfortably*). And is Elizabeth hearty, James?

JAMES (*looking down his nose in the manner proper to young husbands when addressed about their wives*). She's very well, I thank you kindly.

MAGGIE. James is a married man now, Lady Sybil.

> (SYBIL *murmurs her congratulations.*)

JAMES. I thank you kindly. (*Courageously.*)

Yes, I'm married. (*He looks at* DAVID *and* ALICK *to see if they are smiling; and they are.*) It wasn't a case of being catched; it was entirely of my own free will. (*He looks again; and the mean fellows are smiling still.*) Is your ladyship married?

SYBIL. Alas! no.

DAVID. James! (*Politely.*) You will be yet, my lady.

(SYBIL *indicates that he is kind indeed.*)

JOHN. Perhaps they would like you to show them their rooms, Maggie?

DAVID. Fine would we like to see all the house as well as the sleeping accommodation. But first— (*He gives his father the look with which chairmen call on the next speaker.*)

ALICK. I take you, David. (*He produces a paper parcel from a roomy pocket.*) It wasn't likely, Mr. Shand, that we would forget the day.

JOHN. The day?

DAVID. The second anniversary of your marriage. We came purposely for the day.

JAMES (*his fingers itching to take the parcel from his father*). It's a lace shawl, Maggie, from the three of us, a pure Tobermory; you would never dare wear it if you knew the cost.

(*The shawl in its beauty is revealed, and* MAGGIE *hails it with little cries of joy. She rushes at the donors and kisses each of them just as if she were a pretty woman. They are much pleased and give expression to their pleasure in a not very dissimilar manner.*)

ALICK. Havers.

DAVID. Havers.

JAMES. Havers.

JOHN. It 's a very fine shawl.

(*He should not have spoken, for he has set* JAMES's *volatile mind working.*)

JAMES. You may say so. What did you give her, Mr. Shand?

JOHN (*suddenly deserted by God and man*). Me?

ALICK. Yes, yes, let 's see it.

JOHN. Oh—I—

(*He is not deserted by* MAGGIE, *but she can think of no way out.*)

SYBIL (*prompted by the impediment, which is in hiding, quite close*). Did he . . . forget?

(*There is more than a touch of malice in the*

*question. It is a challenge, and the Wylies
as a family are almost too quick to accept a
challenge.)*

MAGGIE (*lifting the gage of battle*). John
forget? Never! It's a pendant, father.

(*The impediment bolts.* JOHN *rises.*)

ALICK. A pendant? One of those things on
a chain?

(*He grins, remembering how once, about
sixty years ago, he and a lady and a pendant—but we have no time for this.*)

MAGGIE. Yes.

DAVID (*who has felt the note of antagonism and
is troubled*). You were slow in speaking of it,
Mr. Shand.

MAGGIE. (*This is her fight.*) He was shy,
because he thought you might blame him for
extravagance.

DAVID (*relieved*). Oh, that's it.

JAMES (*licking his lips*). Let's see it.

MAGGIE (*a daughter of the devil*). Where did
you put it, John?

(JOHN's *mouth opens but has nothing to
contribute.*)

SYBIL (*the impediment has stolen back again*). Perhaps it has been . . . mislaid.

(*The* BROTHERS *echo the word incredulously.*)

MAGGIE. Not it. I can't think where we laid it down, John. It's not on that table, is it, James? (*The Wylies turn to look, and* MAGGIE'S *hand goes out to* LADY SYBIL: JOHN SHAND, *witness. It is a very determined hand, and presently a pendant is placed in it.*) Here it is! (ALICK *and the* BROTHERS *cluster round it, weigh it and appraise it.*)

ALICK. Preserve me. Is that stone real, Mr. Shand?

JOHN (*who has begun to look his grimmest*). Yes.

MAGGIE (*who is now ready, if he wishes it, to take him on too*). John says it's a drop of his blood.

JOHN (*wishing it*). And so it is.

DAVID. Well said, Mr. Shand.

MAGGIE (*scared*). And now, if you'll all come with me, I think John has something he wants to talk over with Lady Sybil. (*Recovering and taking him on.*) Or would you prefer, John, to say it before us all?

SYBIL (*gasping*). No!

JOHN (*flinging back his head*). Yes, I prefer to say it before you all.

MAGGIE (*flinging back hers*). Then sit down again.

(*The Wylies wonderingly obey.*)

SYBIL. Mr. Shand, Mr. Shand!—

JOHN. Maggie knows, and it was only for her I was troubled. Do you think I 'm afraid of *them?* (*With mighty relief.*) Now we can be open.

DAVID (*lowering*). What is it? What 's wrong, John Shand?

JOHN (*facing him squarely*). It was to Lady Sybil I gave the pendant, and all my love with it. (*Perhaps* JAMES *utters a cry, but the silence of* ALICK *and* DAVID *is more terrible.*)

SYBIL (*whose voice is smaller than we had thought*). What are you to do?

(*It is to* MAGGIE *she is speaking.*)

DAVID. She 'll leave it for us to do.

JOHN. That 's what I want.

(*The lords of creation look at the ladies.*)

MAGGIE (*interpreting*). You and I are expected to retire, Lady Sybil, while the men decide our fate. (SYBIL *is ready to obey the law, but* MAGGIE *remains seated.*) Man's the oak, woman's the ivy. Which of us is it that's to cling to you, John?

> (*With three stalwarts glaring at him,* JOHN *rather grandly takes* SYBIL'S *hand. They are two against the world.*)

SYBIL (*a heroine*). I hesitated, but I am afraid no longer; whatever he asks of me I will do.

> (*Evidently the first thing he asks of her is to await him in the dining-room.*)

It will mean surrendering everything for him. I am glad it means all that. (*She passes into the dining-room looking as pretty as a kiss.*)

MAGGIE. So that settles it.

ALICK. I'm thinking that doesn't settle it.

DAVID. No, by God! (*But his love for* MAGGIE *steadies him. There is even a note of entreaty in his voice.*) Have you nothing to say to her, man?

JOHN. I have things to say to her, but not before you.

DAVID (*sternly*). Go away, Maggie. Leave him to us.

JAMES (*who thinks it is about time that he said something*). Yes, leave him to us.

MAGGIE. No, David, I want to hear what is to become of me; I promise not to take any side.

> (*And sitting by the fire she resumes her knitting. The four regard her as on an evening at The Pans a good many years ago.*)

DAVID (*barking*). How long has this been going on?

JOHN. If you mean how long has that lady been the apple of my eye, I 'm not sure; but I never told her of it until to-day.

MAGGIE (*thoughtfully and without dropping a stitch*). I think it wasn't till about six months ago, John, that she began to be very dear to you. At first you liked to bring in her name when talking to me, so that I could tell you of any little things I might have heard she was doing. But afterwards, as she became more and more to you, you avoided mentioning her name.

JOHN (*surprised*). Did you notice that?

MAGGIE (*in her old-fashioned way*). Yes.

JOHN. I tried to be done with it for your sake. I 've often had a sore heart for you, Maggie.

JAMES. You 're proving it!

MAGGIE. Yes, James, he had. I 've often seen him looking at me very sorrowfully of late because of what was in his mind; and many a kindly little thing he has done for me that he didn't used to do.

JOHN. You noticed that too!

MAGGIE. Yes.

DAVID (*controlling himself*). Well, we won't go into that; the thing to be thankful for is that it 's ended.

ALICK (*who is looking very old*). Yes, yes, that 's the great thing.

JOHN. All useless, sir, it 's not ended; it 's to go on.

DAVID. There 's a devil in you, John Shand.

JOHN (*who is an unhappy man just now*). I dare say there is. But do you think he had a walk over, Mr. David?

JAMES. Man, I could knock you down!

MAGGIE. There's not one of you could knock John down.

DAVID (*exasperated*). Quiet, Maggie. One would think you were taking his part.

MAGGIE. Do you expect me to desert him at the very moment that he needs me most?

DAVID. It's him that's deserting you.

JOHN. Yes, Maggie, that's what it is.

ALICK. Where's your marriage vow? And your church attendances?

JAMES (*with terrible irony*). And your prize for moral philosophy?

JOHN (*recklessly*). All gone whistling down the wind.

DAVID. I suppose you understand that you'll have to resign your seat.

JOHN (*his underlip much in evidence*). There are hundreds of seats, but there's only one John Shand.

MAGGIE (*but we don't hear her*). That's how I like to hear him speak.

DAVID (*the ablest person in the room*). Think, man, I'm old by you, and for long I've had a pride in you. It will be beginning the world again with more against you than there was eight years ago.

JOHN. I have a better head to begin it with than I had eight years ago.

ALICK (*hoping this will bite*). She 'll have her own money, David!

JOHN. She 's as poor as a mouse.

JAMES (*thinking possibly of his Elizabeth's mother*). We 'll go to her friends, and tell them all. They 'll stop it.

JOHN. She 's of age.

JAMES. They 'll take her far away.

JOHN. I 'll follow, and tear her from them.

ALICK. Your career—

JOHN (*to his credit*). To hell with my career. Do you think I don't know I 'm on the rocks. What can you, or you, or you, understand of the passions of a man! I 've fought, and I 've given in. When a ship founders, as I suppose I' m foundering, it 's not a thing to yelp at. Peace all of you. (*He strides into the dining-room, where we see him at times pacing the floor.*)

DAVID (*to JAMES, who gives signs of a desire to*

take off his coat). Let him be. We can't budge him. (*With bitter wisdom.*) It 's true what he says, true at any rate about me. What do I know of the passions of a man! I 'm up against something I don't understand.

ALICK. It 's something wicked.

DAVID. I dare say it is, but it 's something big.

JAMES. It 's that damned charm.

MAGGIE (*still by the fire*). That 's it. What was it that made you fancy Elizabeth, James?

JAMES (*sheepishly*). I can scarcely say.

MAGGIE. It was her charm.

DAVID. *Her* charm!

JAMES (*pugnaciously*). Yes, *her* charm.

MAGGIE. She had charm for James.

(*This somehow breaks them up.* MAGGIE *goes from one to another with an odd little smile flickering on her face.*)

DAVID. Put on your things, Maggie, and we 'll leave his house.

MAGGIE (*patting his kind head*). Not me, David.

(*This is a* MAGGIE *they have known but forgotten; all three brighten.*)

DAVID. You haven't given in!

(*The smile flickers and expires.*)

MAGGIE. I want you all to go upstairs, and let me have my try now.

JAMES. Your try?

ALICK. Maggie, you put new life into me.

JAMES. And into me.

(DAVID *says nothing; the way he grips her shoulder says it for him.*)

MAGGIE. I 'll save him, David, if I can.

DAVID. Does he deserve to be saved after the way he has treated you?

MAGGIE. You stupid David. What has that to do with it.

(*When they have gone,* JOHN *comes to the door of the dining-room. There is welling up in him a great pity for* MAGGIE, *but it has to subside a little when he sees that the knitting is still in her hand. No man likes to be so soon supplanted.* SYBIL *follows, and the two of them gaze at the active needles.*)

MAGGIE (*perceiving that she has visitors*). Come in, John. Sit down, Lady Sybil, and make yourself comfortable. I 'm afraid we 've put you about.

> (*She is, after all, only a few years older than they and scarcely looks her age; yet it must have been in some such way as this that the little old woman who lived in a shoe addressed her numerous progeny.*)

JOHN. I 'm mortal sorry, Maggie.

SYBIL (*who would be more courageous if she could hold his hand*). And I also.

MAGGIE (*soothingly*). I 'm sure you are. But as it can't be helped I see no reason why we three shouldn't talk the matter over in a practical way.

> (SYBIL *looks doubtful, but* JOHN *hangs on desperately to the word practical.*)

JOHN. If you could understand, Maggie, what an inspiration she is to me and my work.

SYBIL. Indeed, Mrs. Shand, I think of nothing else.

MAGGIE. That 's fine. That 's as it should be.

SYBIL (*talking too much*). Mrs. Shand, I think you are very kind to take it so reasonably.

MAGGIE. That's the Scotch way. When were you thinking of leaving me, John?

(*Perhaps this is the Scotch way also; but* SYBIL *is English, and from the manner in which she starts you would say that something has fallen on her toes.*)

JOHN (*who has heard nothing fall*). I think, now that it has come to a breach, the sooner the better. (*His tone becomes that of* JAMES *when asked after the health of his wife.*) So long as it is convenient to you, Maggie.

MAGGIE (*making a rapid calculation*). It couldn't well be before Wednesday. That's the day the laundry comes home.

(SYBIL *has to draw in her toes again.*)

JOHN. And it's the day the House rises. (*Stifling a groan.*) It may be my last appearance in the House.

SYBIL (*her arms yearning for him*). No, no, please don't say that.

MAGGIE (*surveying them sympathetically*). You love the House, don't you, John, next to her?

It 's a pity you can't wait till after your speech
at Leeds. Mr. Venables won't let you speak at
Leeds, I fear, if you leave me.

JOHN. What a chance it would have been.
But let it go.

MAGGIE. The meeting is in less than a month.
Could you not make it such a speech that they
would be very loth to lose you?

JOHN (*swelling*). That 's what was in my mind.

SYBIL (*with noble confidence*). And he could
have done it.

MAGGIE. Then we 've come to something
practical.

JOHN (*exercising his imagination with powerful
effect*). No, it wouldn't be fair to you if I was
to stay on now.

MAGGIE. Do you think I 'll let myself be considered when your career is at stake. A month
will soon pass for me; I 'll have a lot of packing
to do.

JOHN. It 's noble of you, but I don't deserve
it, and I can't take it from you.

MAGGIE. Now 's the time, Lady Sybil, for you
to have one of your inspiring ideas.

SYBIL (*ever ready*). Yes, yes—but what?

(*It is odd that they should both turn to* MAGGIE *at this moment.*)

MAGGIE (*who has already been saying it to herself*). What do you think of this: I can stay on here with my father and brothers; and you, John, can go away somewhere and devote yourself to your speech?

SYBIL. Yes.

JOHN. That might be. (*Considerately.*) Away from both of you. Where could I go?

SYBIL (*ever ready*). Where?

MAGGIE. I know.

(*She has called up a number on the telephone before they have time to check her.*)

JOHN (*on his dignity*). Don't be in such a hurry, Maggie.

MAGGIE. Is this Lamb's Hotel? Put me on to the Comtesse de la Brière, please.

SYBIL (*with a sinking*). What do you want with Auntie?

MAGGIE. Her cottage in the country would be the very place. She invited John and me.

JOHN. Yes, but—

MAGGIE (*arguing*). And Mr. Venables is to be there. Think of the impression you could make on *him*, seeing him daily for three weeks.

JOHN.   There 's something in that.

MAGGIE.   Is it you, Comtesse? I 'm Maggie Shand.

SYBIL.   You are not to tell her that—?

MAGGIE.   No. (*To the* COMTESSE.) Oh, I 'm very well, never was better. Yes, yes; you see I can't, because my folk have never been in London before, and I must take them about and show them the sights. But John could come to you alone; why not?

JOHN (*with proper pride*).   If she 's not keen to have me, I won't go.

MAGGIE.   She 's very keen. Comtesse, I could come for a day by and by to see how you are getting on. Yes—yes—certainly. (*To* JOHN.) She says she 'll be delighted.

JOHN (*thoughtfully*).   You 're not doing this, Maggie, thinking that my being absent from Sybil for a few weeks can make any difference? Of course it 's natural you should want us to keep apart, but—

MAGGIE (*grimly.*) I 'm founding no hope on keeping you apart, John.

JOHN. It 's what other wives would do.

MAGGIE. I promised to be different.

JOHN (*his position as a strong man assured*). Then tell her I accept. (*He wanders back into the dining-room.*)

SYBIL. I think—(*she is not sure what she thinks*)—I think you are very wonderful.

MAGGIE. Was that John calling to you?

SYBIL. Was it? (*She is glad to join him in the dining-room.*)

MAGGIE. Comtesse, hold the line a minute— (*She is alone, and she has nearly reached the end of her self-control. She shakes emotionally and utters painful little cries; there is something she wants to do, and she is loth to do it. But she does it.*) Are you there, Comtesse? There 's one other thing, dear Comtesse; I want you to invite Lady Sybil also; yes, for the whole time . that John is there. No, I 'm not mad; as a great favour to me; yes, I have a very particular reason, but I won't tell you what it is; oh, call me Scotchy as much as you like, but consent; do, do, do. Thank you, thank you, good-bye.

> (*She has control of herself now, and is determined not to let it slip from her again. When they reappear the stubborn one is writing a letter.*)

JOHN. I thought I heard the telephone again.

MAGGIE (*looking up from her labours*). It was the Comtesse; she says she 's to invite Lady Sybil to the cottage at the same time.

SYBIL. Me!

JOHN. To invite Sybil? Then of course I won't go, Maggie.

MAGGIE (*wondering seemingly at these niceties.*) What does it matter? Is anything to be considered except the speech? (*It has been admitted that she was a little devil.*) And, with Sybil on the spot, John, *to help you and inspire you*, what a speech it will be!

JOHN (*carried away*). Maggie, you really are a very generous woman.

SYBIL (*convinced at last*). She is indeed.

JOHN. And you 're queer too. How many

women in the circumstances would sit down to write a letter.

MAGGIE. It's a letter to you, John.

JOHN. To me?

MAGGIE. I'll give it to you when it's finished, but I ask you not to open it till your visit to the Comtesse ends.

JOHN. What is it about?

MAGGIE. It's practical.

SYBIL (*rather faintly*). Practical? (*She has heard the word so frequently to-day that it is beginning to have a Scotch sound. She feels she ought to like* MAGGIE, *but that she would like her better if they were farther apart. She indicates that the doctors are troubled about her heart, and murmuring her adieux she goes.* JOHN, *who is accompanying her, pauses at the door.*)

JOHN (*with a queer sort of admiration for his wife*). Maggie, I wish I was fond of you.

MAGGIE (*heartily*). I wish you were, John.

(*He goes, and she resumes her letter. The stocking is lying at hand, and she pushes it to the floor. She is done for a time with knitting.*)

IV

Man's greatest invention is the lawn-mower. All the birds know this, and that is why, when it is at rest, there is always at least one of them sitting on the handle with his head cocked, wondering how the delicious whirring sound is made. When they find out, they will change their note. As it is, you must sometimes have thought that you heard the mower very early in the morning, and perhaps you peeped in négligé from your lattice window to see who was up so early. It was really the birds trying to get the note.

On this broiling morning, however, we are at noon, and whoever looks will see that the whirring is done by Mr. Venables. He is in a linen suit with the coat discarded (the bird is sitting on it), and he comes and goes across the Comtesse's lawns, pleasantly mopping his face. We see him through a crooked bowed window generously open, roses intruding into it as if to prevent its ever being closed at night; there are other roses in such armfuls on the tables that one could not easily say where the room ends and the garden begins.

In the Comtesse's pretty comic drawing-room (for she likes the comic touch when she is in England) sits John Shand with his hostess, on chairs at a great distance from each other. No linen garments for John, nor flannels, nor even knickerbockers; he envies the English way of dressing for trees and lawns, but is too Scotch to be able to imitate it; he wears tweeds, just as he would do in his native country where they would be in kilts. Like many another Scot, the first time he ever saw a kilt was on a Sassenach; indeed kilts were only invented, like golf, to draw the English north. John is doing nothing, which again is not a Scotch accomplishment, and he looks rather miserable and dour. The Comtesse is already at her Patience cards, and occasionally she smiles on him as if not displeased with his long silence. At last she speaks:

'I feel it rather a shame to detain you here on such a lovely day, Mr. Shand, entertaining an old woman.'

'I don't pretend to think I 'm entertaining you, Comtesse.'

'But you *are*, you know.'

'I would be pleased to be told how?'

> (*She shrugs her impertinent shoulders, and presently there is another heavy sigh from* JOHN.)

'Again! Why do not you go out on the river?'

'Yes, I can do that.' (*He rises.*)

'And take Sybil with you.' (*He sits again.*)

'No?'

'I have been on the river with her twenty times.'

'Then take her for a long walk through the Fairloe woods.'

'We were there twice last week.'

'There is a romantically damp little arbour at the end of what the villagers call the Lovers' Lane.'

'One can't go there every day. I see nothing to laugh at.'

'Did I laugh? I must have been translating the situation into French.'

> (*Perhaps the music of the lawn-mower is not to* JOHN'S *mood, for he betakes himself to*

another room. MR. VENABLES *pauses in his labours to greet a lady who has appeared on the lawn, and who is* MAGGIE. *She is as neat as if she were one of the army of typists (who are quite the nicest kind of women), and carries a little bag. She comes in through the window, and puts her hands over the* COMTESSE'S *eyes. The* COMTESSE *says:*

'They are a strong pair of hands, at any rate.'

'And not very white, and biggish for my size. Now guess.'

(The COMTESSE *guesses, and takes both the hands in hers as if she valued them. She pulls off* MAGGIE'S *hat as if to prevent her flying away.)*

'Dear abominable one, not to let me know you were coming.'

'It is just a surprise visit, Comtesse. I walked up from the station.' *(For a moment* MAGGIE *seems to have borrowed* SYBIL'S *impediment.)* How is—everybody?'

'He is quite well. But, my child, he seems to me to be a most unhappy man.'

(*This sad news does not seem to make a
most unhappy woman of the child. The
COMTESSE is puzzled, as she knows nothing
of the situation save what she has dis-
covered for herself.*)

'Why should that please you, O heartless one?'

'I won't tell you.'

'I could take you and shake you, Maggie.
Here have I put my house at your disposal for
so many days for some sly Scotch purpose, and
you will not tell me what it is.'

'No.'

'Very well then, but I have what you call a
nasty one for you. (*The COMTESSE lures MR.
VENABLES into the room by holding up what
might be a foaming glass of lemon squash.*)
Alas, Charles, it is but a flower vase. I want
you to tell Mrs. Shand what you think of her
husband's speech.'

(MR. VENABLES *gives his hostess a reproachful look.*)

'Eh—ah—Shand will prefer to do that himself. I promised the gardener—I must not
disappoint him—excuse me—'

'You must tell her, Charles.'

'Please, Mr. Venables, I should like to know.'

(*He sits down with a sigh and obeys.*)

'Your husband has been writing the speech here, and by his own wish he read it to me three days ago. The occasion is to be an important one; and, well, there are a dozen young men in the party at present, all capable of filling a certain small ministerial post. (*He looks longingly at the mower, but it sends no message to his aid.*) And as he is one of them I was anxious that he should show in this speech of what he is capable.

'And hasn't he?'

(*Not for the first time* MR. VENABLES *wishes that he was not in politics.*)

'I am afraid he has.'

'What is wrong with the speech, Charles?'

'Nothing—and he can still deliver it. It is a powerful, well-thought-out piece of work, such as only a very able man could produce. But it has no *special quality* of its own— none of the little touches that used to make an old stager like myself want to pat Shand on the shoulder. (*The* COMTESSE'S *mouth twitches, but*

MAGGIE *declines to notice it.*) He pounds on manfully enough, but, if I may say so, with a wooden leg. It is as good, I dare say, as the rest of them could have done; but they start with such inherited advantages, Mrs. Shand, that he had to do better.'

'Yes, I can understand that.'

'I am sorry, Mrs. Shand, for he interested me. His career has set me wondering whether if *I* had begun as a railway porter I might not still be calling out, "By your leave." '

(MAGGIE *thinks it probable but not important.*)

'Mr. Venables, now that I think of it, surely John wrote to me that you were dissatisfied with his first speech, and that he was writing another.

(*The* COMTESSE'S *eyes open very wide indeed.*)

'I have heard nothing of that, Mrs. Shand. (VENABLES *shakes his wise head.*) And in any case, I am afraid—' (*He still hears the wooden leg.*)

'But you said yourself that his second thoughts were sometimes such an improvement on the first.'

(The COMTESSE *comes to the help of the baggage.)*

'I remember your saying that, Charles.'

'Yes, that has struck me. *(Politely)* Well, if he has anything to show me— In the mean time—'

(He regains the lawn, like one glad to escape attendance at JOHN's *obsequies. The* COMTESSE *is brought back to speech by the sound of the mower—nothing wooden in it.)*

'What are you up to now, Miss Pin? You know as well as I do that there is no such speech.'

*(*MAGGIE's *mouth tightens.)*

'I do not.'

'It is a duel, is it, my friend?'

(The COMTESSE *rings the bell and* MAGGIE's *guilty mind is agitated.)*

'What are you ringing for?'

'As the challenged one, Miss Pin, I have the choice of weapons. I am going to send for your husband to ask him if he has written such a speech. After which, I suppose, *you* will ask me to leave you while you and he write it together.'

*(*MAGGIE *wrings her hands.)*

'You are wrong, Comtesse; but please don't do that.'

'You but make me more curious, and my doctor says that I must be told everything. (*The* COMTESSE *assumes the pose of her sex in melodrama.*) Put your cards on the table, Maggie Shand, *or*—(*she indicates that she always pinks her man.* MAGGIE *dolefully produces a roll of paper from her bag.*) What precisely is that?'

(*The reply is little more than a squeak.*)

'John's speech.'

'You have written it yourself!'

(MAGGIE *is naturally indignant.*)

'It 's typed.'

'You guessed that the speech he wrote unaided would not satisfy, and you prepared this to take its place!'

'Not at all, Comtesse. It is the draft of his speech that he left at home. That 's all.'

'With a few trivial alterations by yourself, I swear. Can you deny it?'

(*No wonder that* MAGGIE *is outraged. She replaces* JOHN's *speech in the bag with becoming hauteur.*)

'Comtesse, these insinuations are unworthy of you. May I ask where is my husband?'

(*The* COMTESSE *drops her a curtsy.*)

'I believe your Haughtiness may find him in the Dutch garden. Oh, I see through you. You are not to show him your speech. But you are to get him to write another one, and somehow all your additions will be in it. Think not, creature, that you can deceive one so old in iniquity as the Comtesse de la Brière.'

(*There can be but one reply from a good wife to such a charge, and at once the* COMTESSE *is left alone with her shame. Anon a footman appears. You know how they come and go.*)

'You rang, my lady?'

'Did I? Ah, yes, but why? (*He is but lately from the ploughshare and cannot help her. In this quandary her eyes alight upon the bag. She is unfortunately too abandoned to feel her shame: she still thinks that she has the choice of weapons. She takes the speech from the bag and bestows it on her servitor.*) Take this to Mr. Venables, please, and say it is from

Mr. Shand.   (THOMAS—*but in the end we shall probably call him* JOHN—*departs with the little explosive; and when* MAGGIE *returns she finds that the* COMTESSE *is once more engaged on her interrupted game of Patience.*)   You did not find him?'

> (*All the bravery has dropped from* MAGGIE'S *face.*)

'I didn't see him, but I heard him.   *She* is with him.   I think they are coming here.'

> (*The* COMTESSE *is suddenly kind again.*)

'Sybil?   Shall I get rid of her?'

'No, I want her to be here, too.   Now I shall know.'

> (*The* COMTESSE *twists the little thing round.*)

'Know what?'

'As soon as I look into his face I shall know.'

> (*A delicious scent ushers in the fair* SYBIL, *who is as sweet as a milking stool.   She greets* MRS. SHAND *with some alarm.*)

MAGGIE.   How do you do, Lady Sybil?   How pretty you look in that frock.   (SYBIL *rustles uncomfortably.*)   You are a feast to the eye.

SYBIL.   Please, I wish you would not.

(Shall we describe SYBIL'S *frock, in which she looks like a great strawberry that knows it ought to be plucked; or would it be easier to watch the coming of* JOHN*? Let us watch* JOHN*.)*

JOHN. You, Maggie! You never wrote that you were coming.

(No, let us watch MAGGIE. *As soon as she looked into his face she was to know something of importance.)*

MAGGIE *(not dissatisfied with what she sees).* No, John, it's a surprise visit. I just ran down to say good-bye.

(At this his face falls, which does not seem to pain her.)

SYBIL *(foreseeing another horrible Scotch scene).* To say good-bye?

COMTESSE *(thrilling with expectation).* To whom, Maggie?

SYBIL *(deserted by the impediment, which is probably playing with rough boys in the Lovers' Lane).* Auntie, do leave us, won't you?

COMTESSE. Not I. It is becoming far too interesting.

MAGGIE. I suppose there's no reason the Comtesse shouldn't be told, as she will know so soon at any rate?

JOHN. That's so. (SYBIL *sees with a sinking that he is to be practical also.*)

MAGGIE. It's so simple. You see, Comtesse, John and Lady Sybil have fallen in love with one another, and they are to go off as soon as the meeting at Leeds has taken place.

> (*The* COMTESSE's *breast is too suddenly introduced to Caledonia and its varied charms.*)

COMTESSE. Mon Dieu!

MAGGIE. I think that's putting it correctly, John.

JOHN. In a sense. But I'm not to attend the meeting at Leeds. My speech doesn't find favour. (*With a strange humility*) There's something wrong with it.

COMTESSE. I never expected to hear you say that, Mr. Shand.

JOHN (*wondering also*). I never expected it myself. I meant to make it the speech of my career. But somehow my hand seems to have lost its cunning.

COMTESSE. And you don't know how?

JOHN. It 's inexplicable. My brain was never clearer.

COMTESSE. You might have helped him, Sybil.

SYBIL (*quite sulkily*). I did.

COMTESSE. But I thought she was such an inspiration to you, Mr. Shand.

JOHN (*going bravely to* SYBIL's *side*). She slaved at it with me.

COMTESSE. Strange. (*Wickedly becoming practical also.*) So now there is nothing to detain you. Shall I send for a fly, Sybil?

SYBIL (*with a cry of the heart*). Auntie, do leave us.

COMTESSE. I can understand your impatience to be gone, Mr. Shand.

JOHN (*heavily*). I promised Maggie to wait till the 24th, and I 'm a man of my word.

MAGGIE. But I give you back your word, John. You can go now.

(JOHN *looks at* SYBIL, *and* SYBIL *looks at*

JOHN, *and the impediment arrives in time to take a peep at both of them.*)

SYBIL (*groping for the practical, to which we must all come in the end*). He must make satisfactory arrangements about you first. I insist on that.

MAGGIE (*with no more imagination than a hen*). Thank you, Lady Sybil, but I have made all my arrangements.

JOHN (*stung*). Maggie, that was my part.

MAGGIE (*the hens are saying it all the time*). You see, my brothers feel they can't be away from their business any longer; and so, if it would be convenient to you, John, I could travel north with them by the night train on Wednesday.

SYBIL. I—I—. The way you put things—!

JOHN. This is just the 21st.

MAGGIE. My things are all packed. I think you'll find the house in good order, Lady Sybil. I have had the vacuum cleaners in. I'll give you the keys of the linen and the silver plate; I have them in that bag. The carpet on the upper landing is a good deal frayed, but—

SYBIL. Please, I don't want to hear any more.

MAGGIE. The ceiling of the dining-room would be the better of a new lick of paint—

SYBIL (*stamping her foot, small fours*). Can't you stop her?

JOHN (*soothingly*). She's meaning well. Maggie, I know it's natural to you to value those things, because your outlook on life is bounded by them; but all this jars on me.

MAGGIE. Does it?

JOHN. Why should you be so ready to go?

MAGGIE. I promised not to stand in your way.

JOHN (*stoutly*). You needn't be in such a hurry. There are three days to run yet. (*The French are so different from us that we shall probably never be able to understand why the* COMTESSE *laughed aloud here.*) It's just a joke to the Comtesse.

COMTESSE. It seems to be no joke to you, Mr. Shand. Sybil, my pet, are you to let him off?

SYBIL (*flashing*). Let him off? If he wishes it. Do you?

JOHN (*manfully*). I want it to go on. (*Something seems to have caught in his throat: perhaps it is the impediment trying a temporary home.*) It's the one wish of my heart. If you come with me, Sybil, I'll do all in a man's power to make you never regret it.

(*Triumph of the Vere de Veres.*)

MAGGIE (*bringing them back to earth with a dump*). And I can make my arrangements for Wednesday?

SYBIL (*seeking the* COMTESSE'S *protection*). No, you can't. Auntie, I am not going on with this. I'm very sorry for you, John, but I see now—I couldn't face it—

(*She can't face anything at this moment except the sofa pillows.*)

COMTESSE (*noticing* JOHN'S *big sigh of relief*). So *that* is all right, Mr. Shand!

MAGGIE. Don't you love her any more, John? Be practical.

SYBIL (*to the pillows*). At any rate I have tired of him. Oh, best to tell the horrid truth. I am ashamed of myself. I have been crying my eyes out over it—I thought I was such a different kind of woman. But I am weary of him. I think him—oh, so dull.

JOHN (*his face lighting up*). Are you sure that is how you have come to think of me?

SYBIL. I 'm sorry; (*With all her soul*) but yes—yes—yes.

JOHN. By God, it 's more than I deserve.

COMTESSE. Congratulations to you both.

> (SYBIL *runs away; and in the fulness of time she married successfully in Cloth of Silver, which was afterwards turned into a bed-spread.*)

MAGGIE. You haven't read my letter yet, John, have you?

JOHN. No.

COMTESSE (*imploringly*). May I know to what darling letter you refer?

MAGGIE. It 's a letter I wrote to him before he left London. I gave it to him closed, not to be opened until his time here was ended.

JOHN (*as his hand strays to his pocket*). Am I to read it now?

MAGGIE. Not before her. Please go away, Comtesse.

COMTESSE. Every word you say makes me more determined to remain.

MAGGIE. It will hurt you. (*Distressed.*) Don't read it, John; tear it up.

JOHN. You make me very curious, Maggie. And yet I don't see what can be in it.

COMTESSE. But you feel a little nervous? Give *me* the dagger.

MAGGIE (*quickly*). No. (*But the* COMTESSE *has already got it.*)

COMTESSE. May I? (*She must have thought they said Yes, for she opens the letter. She shares its contents with them.*) 'Dearest John, It is at my request that the Comtesse is having Lady Sybil at the cottage at the same time as yourself.'

JOHN. What?

COMTESSE. Yes, she begged me to invite you together.

JOHN. But why?

MAGGIE. I promised you not to behave as other wives would do.

JOHN. It 's not understandable.

COMTESSE. 'You may ask why I do this, John, and my reason is, I think that after a few weeks of Lady Sybil, every day, and all day, you will become sick to death of her. I am also giving her the chance to help you and inspire you with your work, so that you may both learn what her help and her inspiration amount to. Of course, if your love is the great strong passion you think it, then those weeks will make you love her more than ever and I can only say good-bye. But if, as I suspect, you don't even now know what true love is, then by the next time we meet, dear John, you will have had enough of her.—Your affectionate wife, MAGGIE.' Oh, why was not Sybil present at the reading of the will! And now, if you two will kindly excuse me, I think I must go and get that poor sufferer the eau de Cologne.

JOHN. It 's almost enough to make a man lose faith in himself.

COMTESSE. Oh, don't say that, Mr. Shand.

MAGGIE (*defending him*). You mustn't hurt him. If you haven't loved deep and true, that 's just because you have never met a woman yet, John, capable of inspiring it.

COMTESSE (*putting her hand on* MAGGIE'S *shoulder*). Have you not, Mr. Shand?

JOHN. I see what you mean. But Maggie

wouldn't think better of me for any false pretences. She knows my feelings for her now are neither more nor less than what they have always been.

MAGGIE (*who sees that he is looking at her as solemnly as a volume of sermons printed by request*). I think no one could be fond of me that can't laugh a little at me.

JOHN. How could that help?

COMTESSE (*exasperated*). Mr. Shand, I give you up.

MAGGIE. I admire his honesty.

COMTESSE. Oh, I give you up also. Arcades ambo. Scotchies both.

JOHN (*when she has gone*). But this letter, it's not like you. By Gosh, Maggie, you're no fool.

(*She beams at this, as any wife would.*)

But how could I have made such a mistake? It's not like a strong man. (*Evidently he has an inspiration.*)

MAGGIE. What is it?

JOHN (*the inspiration*). *Am* I a strong man?

MAGGIE. You? Of course you are. And

self made. Has anybody ever helped you in the smallest way?

JOHN (*thinking it out again*). No, nobody.

MAGGIE. Not even Lady Sybil?

JOHN. I 'm beginning to doubt it. It 's very curious, though, Maggie, that this speech should be disappointing.

MAGGIE. It 's just that Mr. Venables hasn't the brains to see how good it is.

JOHN. That must be it. (*But he is too good a man to rest satisfied with this.*) No, Maggie, it 's not. Somehow I seem to have lost my neat way of saying things.

MAGGIE (*almost cooing*). It will come back to you.

JOHN (*forlorn*). If you knew how I 've tried.

MAGGIE (*cautiously*). Maybe if you were to try again; and I 'll just come and sit beside you, and knit. I think the click of the needles sometimes put you in the mood.

JOHN. Hardly that; and yet many a Shandism have I knocked off while you were sitting beside me knitting. I suppose it was the quietness.

MAGGIE. Very likely.

JOHN (*with another inspiration*). Maggie!

MAGGIE (*again*). What is it, John?

JOHN. What if it was you that put those queer ideas into my head!

MAGGIE. Me?

JOHN. Without your knowing it, I mean.

MAGGIE. But how?

JOHN. We used to talk bits over; and it may be that you dropped the seed, so to speak.

MAGGIE. John, could it be this, that I sometimes had the idea in a rough womanish sort of way and then you polished it up till it came out a Shandism?

JOHN (*slowly slapping his knee*). I believe you 've hit it, Maggie: to think that you may have been helping me all the time—and neither of us knew it.

> (*He has so nearly reached a smile that no one can say what might have happened within the next moment if the* COMTESSE *had not reappeared.*)

COMTESSE. Mr. Venables wishes to see you, Mr. Shand.

WHAT EVERY WOMAN KNOWS 155

JOHN (*lost, stolen, or strayed a smile in the making*). Hum.

COMTESSE. He is coming now.

JOHN (*grumpy*). Indeed.

COMTESSE (*sweetly*). It is about your speech.

JOHN. He has said all he need say on that subject, and more.

COMTESSE (*quaking a little*). I think it is about the second speech.

JOHN. What second speech?

(MAGGIE *runs to her bag and opens it.*)

MAGGIE (*horrified*). Comtesse, you have given it to him.

COMTESSE (*impudently*). Wasn't I meant to?

JOHN. What is it? What second speech?

MAGGIE. Cruel, cruel. (*Willing to go on her knees.*) You had left the first draft of your speech at home, John, and I brought it here with —with a few little things I 've added myself.

JOHN (*a seven-footer*). What 's that?

MAGGIE (*four foot ten at most*). Just trifles— things I was to suggest to you—while I was knitting—and then, if you liked any of them you could have polished them—and turned them into something good. John, John—and now she has shown it to Mr. Venables.

JOHN (*thundering*). As my work, Comtesse?
(*But the* COMTESSE *is not of the women who are afraid of thunder.*)

MAGGIE. It is your work—nine-tenths of it.

JOHN (*in the black cap*). You presumed, Maggie Shand! Very well, then, here he comes, and now we 'll see to what extent you 've helped me.

VENABLES. My dear fellow. My dear Shand, I congratulate you. Give me your hand.

JOHN. The speech?

VENABLES. You have improved it out of knowledge. It is the same speech, but those new touches make all the difference. (JOHN *sits down heavily.*) Mrs. Shand, be proud of him.

MAGGIE. I am. I am, John.

COMTESSE. You always said that his second thoughts were best, Charles.

VENABLES (*pleased to be reminded of it*). Didn't I? didn't I? Those delicious little touches! How good that is, Shand, about the flowing tide.

COMTESSE. The flowing tide?

VENABLES. In the first speech it was something like this—'Gentlemen, the Opposition are calling to you to vote for them and the flowing tide, but I solemnly warn you to beware lest the flowing tide does not engulf you.' The second way is much better.

COMTESSE. What is the second way, Mr. Shand?

(JOHN *does not tell her.*)

VENABLES. This is how he puts it now. (JOHN *cannot help raising his head to listen.*) 'Gentlemen, the Opposition are calling to you to vote for them and the flowing tide, but I ask you cheerfully to vote for us and *dam* the flowing tide.'

(VENABLES *and his old friend the* COMTESSE *laugh heartily, but for different reasons.*)

COMTESSE. It *is* better, Mr. Shand.

MAGGIE. *I* don't think so.

VENABLES. Yes, yes, it's so virile. Excuse me, Comtesse, I'm off to read the whole thing again. (*For the first time he notices that* JOHN *is strangely quiet.*) I think this has rather bowled you over, Shand.

(JOHN'S *head sinks lower.*)

Well, well, good news doesn't kill.

MAGGIE (*counsel for the defence*). Surely the important thing about the speech is its strength and knowledge and eloquence, the things that were in the first speech as well as in the second.

VENABLES. That of course is largely true. The wit would not be enough without them, just as they were not enough without the wit. It is the combination that is irresistible. (JOHN's *head rises a little.*) Shand, you are our man, remember that, it is emphatically 'the best thing you have ever done. How this will go down at Leeds.

> (*He returns gaily to his hammock; but lower sinks* JOHN's *head, and even the* COMTESSE *has the grace to take herself off.* MAGGIE'S *arms flutter near her husband, not daring to alight.*)

'You heard what he said, John. It 's the combination. Is it so terrible to you to find that my love for you had made me able to help you in the little things?'

'The little things! It seems strange to me to hear you call me by my name, Maggie. It 's as if I looked on you for the first time.'

'Look at me, John, for the first time. What do you see?'

'I see a woman who has brought her husband low.'

'Only that?'

'I see the tragedy of a man who has found himself out. Eh, I can't live with you again, Maggie.'

(*He shivers.*)

'Why did you shiver, John?'

'It was at myself for saying that I couldn't live with you again, when I should have been wondering how for so long you have lived with me. And I suppose you have forgiven me all the time. (*She nods.*) And forgive me still? (*She nods again.*) Dear God!'

'John, am I to go? or are you to keep me on? (*She is now a little bundle near his feet.*) I'm willing to stay because I'm useful to you, if it can't be for a better reason. (*His hand feels for her, and the bundle wriggles nearer.*) It's nothing unusual I've done, John. Every man who is high up loves to think that he has done it all himself; and the wife smiles, and lets it go at that. It 's our only joke. Every woman knows that. (*He stares at her in hopeless perplexity.*) Oh, John, if only you could laugh at me.'

'I can't laugh, Maggie.'

> (*But as he continues to stare at her a strange disorder appears in his face.* MAGGIE *feels that it is to be now or never.*)

'Laugh, John, laugh. Watch me; see how easy it is.'

> (*A terrible struggle is taking place within him. He creaks. Something that may be mirth forces a passage, at first painfully, no more joy in it than in the discoloured water from a spring that has long been dry. Soon, however, he laughs loud and long. The spring water is becoming clear.* MAGGIE *claps her hands. He is saved.*)

THE END

Printed in the United Kingdom
by Lightning Source UK Ltd.
109343UKS00002B/234